How Big Should Our Government Be?

How Big Should Our Government Be?

Jon Bakija, Lane Kenworthy,
Peter Lindert, and Jeff Madrick

UNIVERSITY OF CALIFORNIA PRESS

University of California Press, one of the most distinguished university presses in the United States, enriches
lives around the world by advancing scholarship in the
humanities, social sciences, and natural sciences. Its
activities are supported by the UC Press Foundation and
by philanthropic contributions from individuals and
institutions. For more information, visit www.ucpress.edu.

University of California Press
Oakland, California

Library of Congress Cataloging-in-Publication Data

Names: Bakija, Jon M., author. | Kenworthy, Lane,
    author. | Lindert, Peter H., author. | Madrick, Jeffrey
    G., author.
Title: How big should our government be? /Jon Bakija,
    Lane Kenworthy, Peter Lindert, and Jeff Madrick
Description: Oakland, California : University of
    California Press, [2016] | Includes bibliographical
    references and index
Identifiers: LCCN 2015044265 (print) | LCCN 2016012363
    (ebook) | ISBN 9780520291829 (pbk. : alk. paper) |
    ISBN 9780520962811 (ebook) | ISBN 9780520291829
    (pbk : alk. paper)
Subjects: LCSH: Government spending policy—United
    States. | United States—Economic conditions. | United
    States—Economic policy. | United States—Social
    policy. | United States—Politics and government.
Classification: LCC HJ7537 .M33 2016 (print) | LCC HJ7537
    (ebook) | DDC 336.3/90973—dc23
LC record available at http://lccn.loc.gov/2015044265

25 24 23 22 21 20 19 18 17 16
10 9 8 7 6 5 4 3 2 1

CONTENTS

Preface vii

1. Can Government Help? 1

2. Are Government Social Programs
   Bad for Economic Growth? 34

3. Would a Bigger Government Hurt
   the Economy? 67

4. Thinking Sensibly about the Size of
   Government 135

Notes 145

References 171

Index 199

PREFACE

Just after he was elected president in 2008, Barack Obama called for a bipartisan deficit commission to develop a set of recommendations to restore "fiscal responsibility" to the nation. At the time, the budget deficit of 10 percent had alarmed the country and balancing the budget became a national goal. Reducing the deficit has continued to be a major issue in American political life, and there has been a huge amount of misinformed national attention paid to this subject.

In fact, the deficit was overwhelmingly caused by the stunning collapse of national income due to the recession of 2008, not by government spending. However, it was a small matter to the public discourse that, if the cause of the deficit was a reduction in tax revenues, the cure was to raise the national economy from recessionary levels and grow it again. Because even President Obama apparently agreed that government expenditure was significantly to blame for the deficit, there was only modest debate over the issue. National anger and alarm focused on reducing federal spending, which was a demand that had been simmering since the 1970s and had finally reached a boiling point. Obama's National Commission on Fiscal Responsibility and Reform focused its attention on sharply cutting government spending, both in the short term and in the long term.

This brief book is a response to the poorly informed national debate over the size of government. As its authors, we hope to broaden the nation's understanding of how big government actually should be by presenting the best research on the subject.

The glaringly misinformed recommendation of the Obama commission was to reduce federal spending to 21 percent of gross domestic product (GDP). Federal spending had spiked to about 25 percent at the depth of the recession, while federal tax revenues had collapsed to about 15 percent of GDP. The 21 percent ceiling the commission proposed was not based on any serious economic or historical analysis. The two chairs of the commission, Erskine Bowles, a Democrat who had served as president Clinton's chief of staff, and Alan Simpson, a conservative Republican who had retired from the Senate in 1997, had no serious training in economics. The eighteen members of the commission were almost all members of Congress.

The rationale Bowles and Simpson gave for the 21 percent ceiling was that this had been the average level of federal government spending as a proportion of GDP since 1970. Yet such a straitjacket makes no sense. In the coming years, the nation's citizens will get older, so Social Security and Medicare will necessarily become more costly. The government has adopted a drug plan for seniors. Its infrastructure needs are soaring. A growing consensus demands pre-K for all children. And it is spending enormous sums on homeland security. Government spending has to grow to meet these and other basic needs.

To be sure, there were somewhat cooler and better-informed analyses. A second commission, sponsored by the new Bipartisan Policy Center, which was created by former Senate majority leaders, proposed a higher ceiling for spending and suggested raising more in taxes than the Obama commission did. But this commission's proposals were also limited by politics. A third commission, sponsored by the National Academy of Sciences, was better grounded but still abided by limits on government that aren't justified by serious research.

A national instinct that small government is always better than large government is grounded not in facts but rather in ideology and politics. Over the years since the Obama commission was created, opposition to so-called big government policies has continued. The federal deficit fell from 10 percent to 3 percent as the economy grew, yet cries to reduce government were undiminished. The Committee for a Responsible Federal Budget was probably the most prominent of the foundations dedicated to frightening America into reducing its spending, and to this day it continues to warn the nation to cut social programs, notably Social Security and Medicare. Small government is a campaign centerpiece for most of the candidates running for the Republican Party's 2016 presidential nomination.

As the reader will see in the following pages, the very history of America, a country whose skepticism of government lies deep in its national character, should rebut fears that the government would grow too large. The federal government adopted new responsibilities throughout America's history, and its size grew with no appreciable effect on the economy. It levied progressive taxes and payroll taxes as well as sales taxes, and prosperity has increased at the same historically rapid rate since the late 1800s, interrupted only by business cycles.

The need for more government to help us maintain a just society and a prosperous economy becomes more evident by the day. Today more than ever before, low-income Americans are more dependent for their survival on government social programs. Education, infrastructure, technology and research, financial and safety regulations, and job creation will all require more government investment in the future. Spouses need programs to allow them to work while they raise children. Our high level of poverty, especially child poverty, is a stain on the nation.

The Obama commission produced a political document, not an economic one. Since Obama has been in office, political candidates have followed his lead. Calls for austerity have set the tone for the nation's policies. But America cannot allow itself to be inhibited by political claims disguised as economic truths. It can afford to meet the needs of its citizens.

This doesn't mean that government is being run perfectly or that all programs and even agencies should be kept. It doesn't mean that government can solve every problem. What it does mean is that the nation should not be deterred from doing what it believes must be done by an artificial, politically contrived limit on government's size. The evidence shows that more government can lead to greater security, enhanced opportunity, and a fairer sharing of national wealth, and this is the case throughout the history of modern capitalism.

We present the evidence in the following pages. We hope to influence both the political discourse and Americans themselves. Myths perpetuated by defunct ideologies and economic crises can profoundly damage a nation and its future.

Jeff Madrick

CHAPTER ONE

Can Government Help?

LANE KENWORTHY AND JEFF MADRICK

The size of government is the most fundamental axis of political disagreement in the United States. It has played a significant role since the Jeffersonian era and has been at the heart of American politics for the past eighty years, since the New Deal programs of the 1930s. It won't fade from prominence any time soon, regardless of how ongoing debates about government debt, entitlement reform, and taxes play out.

Much of the contemporary American right, along with many nominally centrist deficit hawks, insist that our government is too big. They want it to shrink.

We believe it ought to be bigger, and if Americans can shed themselves of the baggage of the past thirty years of public discourse, we believe they will agree. Imagine how a proposal for the New Deal would have been received if it had been put forward in the 1920s. A decade later, however, it was common sense. A similar new and vigorous extension of government, along with higher taxes to finance it, is now needed in the United States.

There are four areas where a bigger government can help. First, America has been underinvesting in infrastructure. To maintain our economic strength and assure continued improvement in living standards, we need to boost funding for this vital public good.

Second, as the country continues to get richer, Americans, like their counterparts in other affluent nations, will want more insurance against risk—more economic security. We have commitments to the elderly for cash transfers and medical care that will require increased spending in coming decades. Beyond this, we'll want to expand some existing programs, such as unemployment insurance, Medicare and Medicaid, and individualized assistance for the disadvantaged, disabled, and displaced. And we'll want to add others, including paid sick leave, paid parental leave, and wage insurance.

Third, we have a large opportunity deficit. Americans who grow up in low-income families face long odds of rising into the middle class. This violation of equal opportunity, which has long been one of the nation's most cherished aims, begs a renewed effort to improve and expand schooling and to provide more resources and programs for less-advantaged children in their most malleable years, zero to five.

Fourth, as wages have stagnated, too little of the economy's growth has gone to middle- and low-income households. Experience here and abroad since the 1970s suggests that wages for people in the bottom half of earners are unlikely to increase in the absence of strong unions or sustained full employment. A helpful alternative, or complement, to rising wages would be to broaden eligibility for the existing Earned Income Tax Credit so that it benefits not just the working poor but also much of the middle class, and to tie it to GDP per capita so that the amount of the credit rises in sync with the economy.

Given the state of contemporary American politics, the notion of increasing government spending (as a share of GDP) may seem radical or utopian. But it is neither. The expectation of a larger government in the future follows directly from our history and from that of other rich nations.

THE MYTH OF LAISSEZ-FAIRE AMERICA

America was never a nation of laissez-faire economic policies, though it has often told itself it was—and continues to do so. The myth goes further. It claims that laissez-faire sentiments are what made America great, keeping government out of the way, making people self-reliant, and allowing individualism to prove its benefits.

This self-identifying myth is largely wrong. Government was always a strong force in the United States, even in colonial years—serving both as a key to true freedom and economic prosperity and, at times, as an obstacle to it.

For all the talk of the advantages of small government in America, even politicians such as Thomas Jefferson, who warned of the dangers of big government, fortunately never really practiced what they preached. In the beginning, America's prosperity was mostly dependent on its abundant land, which was especially important in an agrarian age. In the United States, owning arable land was the source of independence. If you could feed yourself, you could be free. Remarkably, scholars estimate that well over half of early Americans owned their own land around 1800.[1]

However, much of the distribution of land was controlled or made possible by government. The colonies themselves owned most of the land to their west, having confiscated it from giant landlords after the Revolution. When the United States was formed, a key concession the colonies made was donating their land to the federal government, which became the largest owner of land in the nation. Soon enough, partly because of Jefferson, rules and regulations were adopted for the sale of that land. Some rules were designed to make the price relatively cheap to facilitate land ownership.

There were countless regulations on the prices and sales of products in early America as well, which might surprise contemporary readers. Many from the Old World immigrated to the new land as indentured servants and had to win their freedom. How poorly America's history is understood through myths that cannot see beyond markets and that neglect the central role government has historically played.[2]

Two early events in the nation's history fully qualify as the actions of "big government" by any historical standard. Defying the US Constitution, Jefferson bought the Louisiana Territory from France, which roughly doubled the size of the young nation. This was partly a decision made to secure the country's borders, but it was at least equally, if not more so, an economic decision to enable Americans to buy land for themselves at cheap prices for as far as the eye could see and as long as the imagination could conjure.

In the meantime, Jefferson's nemesis, Alexander Hamilton, insisted the United States start a national bank, in opposition to political forces that feared centralized government. He also insisted the nation borrow money. In fact, Jefferson had borrowed money to make the Louisiana Purchase.

Hamilton went further, of course. He supported tariffs to protect budding manufacturing and also promoted loans for new business. Today, we call such measures industrial policy. Today's right firmly opposes industrial policy, as do even some left-leaning economists.[3] Yet Hamilton fully supported it. A tariff passed, ironically, under James Madison, Jefferson's Republican successor and an author of *The Federalist Papers.*

In the fog of mythmaking, one of the most important purposes of government goes unstated: government is a key agent of change. America became what it is today by adjusting constructively to a radically changing economy, new social ideas, and rising expectations of security and fairness. On balance, the nation reacted well to change. But it didn't always do so, and it often took a long time to make the right decisions. Political battles to limit government's role in adapting to new needs were persistent. Sometimes checks on power were needed, to be sure. But delays in public investment, social reform, and central banking held the nation back. Fortunately, most of the time America eventually righted itself and recognized and implemented the constructive uses of government. Yet too often it did not do enough—or do it quickly enough. We grew nevertheless, including in the twentieth century, when government spending as a proportion of the economy rose most rapidly.

But let's step back to conjure up again the history of the last 250 years. Jefferson and Hamilton enabled and supported change by making government bigger. This didn't manifest in more government spending, as it does today, but as regulations, land purchases, tariffs, and borrowing.

None of the founding fathers could have anticipated what was to come. The rapid commercialization of the economy changed America in the early 1800s. Trade of agricultural goods within the nation and exports overseas required roadways and canals. The federal government unfortunately resisted the requests to build this infrastructure, but the states took up the call. Members of Jefferson's own party in New York State started building the Erie Canal, mostly with funds from state-financed borrowing. The canal was operating by 1825, and many other states followed suit. Trade across America and exports to foreign markets boomed.[4]

The federal government provided financing for roads during the presidency of John Quincy Adams. But, despite the efforts of John Calhoun and Henry Clay, Congress demurred. Had it not, American development would have proceeded more rapidly. In the 1800s, the states generally compensated, albeit late and less than adequately, for what the federal government failed to do.

The development of the canals in many states—including, notably, Maryland, Massachusetts, and Pennsylvania—was a major achievement. But the greatest achievement of the states was creating a primary education system that was free and mandatory. The rapid development of free public education in America was extraordinary. Massachusetts led the way, having made primary schooling mandatory by the late 1820s. Although it is rarely seen as such, primary schooling in America was the first great income distribution plan in the United States, as primary education was financed by property taxes and rich and poor alike attended. By 1850 or so, America spent as much per child on education as France or Prussia and had about as many children enrolled as a proportion of the population as either of those European leaders. The nation was only sixty years old. This was among the great accomplishments of the young government. To this day, states do most K-12 education financing in America, and one of the results of this system is that the financing of K-12 is highly unequal. Had the federal government been more active in investing in education and maintaining its quality in the 1800s, America's K-12 schooling arguably would be more effective and provide more equal services today.

After the Civil War, industrialization again changed America, perhaps more radically than ever before or since. There were countless new demands on society. As big business—oil, steel, retailing, and more—boomed, the federal government financed much of the development of the nation's railroads through donations of its vast land holdings. Corruption and waste characterized railroad development, but the amount of track laid was astonishing. The speed and reach of the railroads made a national marketplace possible, enabling business to fully exploit economies of scale in producing oil, steel, and other mass-produced products. Transportation infrastructure was key to development in this era.

Meanwhile, the government set aside land for agricultural and technical colleges under the 1853 Morrill Act, a favorite of Abraham Lincoln's. The land was donated to the schools, which could in turn sell it to finance themselves. This is how UC Berkeley, MIT, Texas A&M, and Ohio State, among many others, got their start.

And let's not forget the postal system. Postal boxes soon dotted street corners in cities across America.

Little of this showed up as government spending, but it was big government nevertheless. If the value of the land given away had been measured, it would have been clear that America already had a large government by standards of the day in the late 1800s.

It was also clear by then that political power in America was being consolidated in Washington. The Civil War did not end discrimination against blacks, but it did result in the rise of a centralized federal government—Lincoln's dream.

Industrialization, as noted, brought a radical change to life in America. Land was no longer the single source of self-esteem and independence. Now a job was. But there weren't enough jobs, and they typically didn't pay adequately. Working conditions were often inhumane. Children and women worked long hours.

At the same time, the phenomenon of involuntary unemployment appeared, which was something new in America. Though many balked at the idea that anyone could be unemployed, historians say the unemployment rate in these years reached up to 15 percent. But until the 1890s, America was slow to use government to reform and control business. Social Darwinism influenced the nation's attitudes—there was a belief that people should be self-reliant and that the strong would rise from the pack.

By the late 1800s and early 1900s, however, political attitudes again turned toward constructive uses of government. Antitrust laws were passed, and a new federal commission was created to control commerce across state lines. Reforms were underway to limit work hours, prevent child labor, and oversee product quality. One wonders how the invisible hand would have solved these problems over time had the government not interceded.

One widely overlooked but critical area of federal, state, and local intervention was sanitation. During industrialization, cities boomed and overcrowding resulted in unhealthy conditions. Life spans were far shorter in the cities than in the countryside. Above all, as was widely understood by then, water had to be purified and streets had to be cleaned. In the 1850s, a contaminated water source in London caused a cholera epidemic, and the story was reported around the world. Private enterprise did not sanitize America; the government did. In fact, the best water purification methods were developed by chemists in the US Army in the early 1900s, and these discoveries are still the basis of water purification today. Sound familiar? The Internet, to take but one well-known example, was originally developed in the US Department of Defense.

American states and cities were the leaders in developing sanitation. Indeed, the late 1800s and early 1900s became known as "the age of sanitation."[5] Cities could not have expanded and advanced without these innovations. New York, the greatest city of the era and the hub of American trade, had clean running water and widespread indoor plumbing before any other major city. It also had a clean street campaign before others did. American cities themselves then became critical engines of economic growth, creating efficient pockets of demand, manufacturing, and marketing.

Economic development became more complex in the twentieth century. Booms and busts had taken too big a toll. The first nationwide financial crash and recession occurred in 1819, but there were others, and they grew worse. J.P. Morgan famously refinanced America after the devastating Panic of 1907, but it was clear a government central bank was needed (Andrew Jackson vetoed renewal legislation for the first one). The Federal Reserve (commonly known as the Fed) was created in 1913, and, although it took time to make it operate smoothly, the institution became critical to later finance and stability, if not free of controversy.

America went through political cycles of pro- and antigovernment sentiments. In the 1920s, antigovernment attitudes prevailed, similar to what had happened in the post–Civil War era. Free enterprise and unregulated finance were in vogue. It was a decade of consumer transformation. Cars, electricity, refrigerators, washing machines, radios, and cinema became widespread. Mass production was perfected by Henry Ford and others. Mass marketing also flourished, especially with the advent of nationwide radio. But unfettered capitalism proved itself to be incapable of self-management. The 1929 crash and the Great Depression made its immense vulnerabilities and excesses manifest.

The federal government under President Franklin D. Roosevelt not only cleaned up much of that mess but also created rules and regulations that would foster stability and prosperity, bring about rising wages and technological advance, and produce the nation's first true middle class. In the 1930s, the government regulated finance through the Securities and Exchange Commission, created Social Security, developed jobs programs, introduced unemployment insurance, provided insurance for deposits in banks, and passed laws enabling labor unions to organize. All these measures were reactions to a radically changing economy.

Would the United States have surged forward to become one of the world's leading economic powerhouses without the New Deal? Not likely, but a lively and, in light of America's history, sometimes dispiriting economic debate arose about government intervention. The British economist John Maynard Keynes provided a framework for justifying government budget deficits to raise growth rates to optimal levels. Between 1933 and 1937, growth soared. But then President Roosevelt succumbed to old ideas about balanced budgets and retreated on stimulus, and at the same time, the Fed tightened money. A new recession devastated the country.

An economic debate escalated over whether government intervention was beneficial or detrimental.[6] Spending for World War II raised the nation from recession, but would that be considered a Keynesian stimulus or a large-scale redevelopment and modernization of the nation's productive capacity?[7] At the very least, history made clear that there was no period of true laissez-faire policy in America that could support the new extremist claims made by economists known as the "new classicals," led initially by Nobelist Robert Lucas of the University of Chicago, who argued that the only impediment to prosperity was government itself.

In the post–World War II period, an evolving economy again created new needs. State governments had built high schools in the late 1800s and early 1900s, and high school graduation rates soared. It was now clear that Americans ought to go to college. The GI Bill put hundreds of thousands of veterans through higher education, and loan and grant programs were developed to help a new generation get a university education.

The new transportation needs of the nation were met by President Eisenhower's highway system. But even he had to sell this vast infrastructure program to Congress as a national security defense plan.

It also became clear that great gaps in social welfare had formed. The elderly did not receive sufficient retirement benefits, so Social Security was expanded. In 1965, Medicare was created to provide for the health of those sixty-five and over. Michael Harrington, in his classic early-1960s book *The Other America,* brought attention to the unconscionable poverty rates in the world's richest nation. Medicaid was created to provide healthcare to poor families, and new antipoverty programs like Food Stamps were developed. The federal government addressed racial discrimination with the Voting Rights Act and the Civil Rights Act, though attempts to pass an equal rights amendment for women failed.

The backlash against government that began in the late 1970s did not seriously address American history. It was a movement largely led by economic theorists who claimed high taxes and big government reduced growth, and it evolved into the extremist views of the new classicals, who believed that, left on its own, a free market economy would pay people fairly, be stable, and maximize prosperity for all. That hasn't turned out to be the case.

America today is once again behind in dealing with a changing world. Four major areas of neglect—infrastructure, economic security, equality of opportunity, and fairly shared prosperity—require expansion of government efforts.

INFRASTRUCTURE

Infrastructure underpins a successful economy. American firms and citizens face significant hurdles and risks due to our failure to maintain and improve our roads, bridges, plane and rail systems, city layouts, broadband networks, and water systems. The American Society of Civil Engineers reports that one-third of US roads are in poor or mediocre condition. According to the Federal Highway Administration, one-quarter of America's bridges are deficient or functionally obsolete. The cost of traffic congestion in fuel and lost time is estimated to be nearly 1 percent of GDP. Delayed and canceled plane flights cost another 0.25 percent of GDP. We have an efficient freight-rail system for transporting products, but high-speed rail to move people around is nonexistent. The current California drought has exposed, once again, the inadequacy of our water supply systems. Four thousand dams are in need of repair. And in 2015, 15 percent of Americans reported that they do not use the Internet, and one-third lacked access to a high-speed connection.[8]

This isn't to say that America's infrastructure is worse than it used to be. That fairly common assertion is based largely on anecdote.[9] Nor is it to suggest that our infrastructure is far behind that of other affluent nations. We do lag behind some of them, according to the most recent assessment by the World Economic

Forum, but the gap isn't enormous.[10] The point, rather, is that our infrastructure isn't as good as it could and should be.

Investment in infrastructure is doubly beneficial in that it not only greases the wheels of the economy but also increases employment.[11] It thereby helps to address the problems of inadequate economic security, opportunity, and shared prosperity that we discuss later in this chapter.

The amounts of money needed to resolve this problem aren't huge. One proposal, from a progressive think tank, estimates that bringing our road, bridge, mass transit, rail, port, airport, inland waterway, drinking water, wastewater, and energy infrastructure up to par would require additional expenditures by the federal government of about 0.5 percent of GDP per year.[12]

Although the 2009 American Recovery and Reinvestment Act allocated considerable funds for infrastructure, those funds were short-term. Given that interest rates have been very low in recent years, we've missed a terrific opportunity to more aggressively boost infrastructure investment. But it's not too late.

ECONOMIC SECURITY

To be economically secure is to have sufficient resources to cover one's expenses. The chief threats to economic security are low income, unstable income, and unexpected large expenses.[13]

From the 1930s through the mid-1970s, economic security increased for most Americans.[14] Household incomes up and down the socioeconomic ladder grew steadily, reducing the percentage of people in poverty and enabling the purchase of various types of insurance. Homeownership increased, providing an asset cushion for the growing middle class. An array of government programs—limited liability law, bankruptcy protection,

Social Security old-age benefits, unemployment insurance, the statutory minimum wage, Aid to Families with Dependent Children (AFDC, which later became Temporary Assistance for Needy Families [TANF]), Social Security disability benefits and Supplemental Security Income (SSI), Medicare, Medicaid, food stamps, the Earned Income Tax Credit, disaster relief, and others—shielded Americans from devastating financial risks.[15]

A generation later, we've made little further progress, and in some respects, things have gotten worse. As of 2013, the average income of the roughly 25 million households in the bottom 20 percent (quintile) was just $19,500.[16] While very few of these low-income Americans are destitute—most have clothing, food, and shelter and many have a car, a television, heat and air conditioning, and access to medical care[17]—making ends meet on an income of $19,500 is difficult.[18] Many of these households are barely scraping by, and some make do on incomes that are appallingly low.[19] Moreover, there has been little improvement in the past generation. Between 1979 and 2013, average income among households in the bottom fifth rose by just $1,500.[20]

Instability of household income is another aspect of economic insecurity. Estimates by a number of researchers suggest that in any given year, 10 to 20 percent of working-age American households will experience an income decline of 25 percent or more,[21] and about twice that number will experience this kind of income drop from one year to the next at some point over a period of ten years.[22] The incidence of these large year-to-year income declines has increased since the late 1970s.[23]

Instability *within* a year also can put a strain on households.[24] For some, work hours vary from month to month as one or more adults in the household move between jobs or take time off due to sickness or family constraints. And some types of employment—such as seasonal jobs, temp work, and "sharing economy" positions—are inherently irregular. Even when employment is stable, pay can vary. This has always been true for taxi drivers and waitresses, but uncertain pay is becoming more common in other occupations.

A sharp drop in a person's income causes economic insecurity because they may then have trouble meeting their expenses. A large unanticipated expense can produce the same result.[25] In the United States, the most common large unexpected expenses are medical. The 2010 health care reform is expected to reduce the share of uninsured Americans to perhaps 7 to 8 percent, down from 16 percent in the year the law was passed. That will be a significant accomplishment, reversing the trend of recent decades, but it will leave us well short of where we should be.

It isn't only the uninsured who are insecure. Some Americans have a health insurance policy that is inadequate. Each year, 25 to 30 percent of Americans say they or a member of their family have put off medical treatment because of the extra cost they would have to pay.[26]

Most other rich nations, particularly the Nordic countries, do better at ensuring economic security. In these nations, households on the low rungs of the socioeconomic ladder have higher incomes than their American counterparts, fewer households lack basic necessities or are unable to pay their regular bills, fewer suffer a sharp drop in household income if earnings from work decrease or disappear, and fewer face the prospect of getting hit with a large unexpected medical bill. Government policy plays a key role in achieving these outcomes.[27]

What can we do to enhance economic security in the United States? For people with jobs, we can address the problem of low household income via two steps. One is to increase the statutory minimum wage and index it to inflation. The other is to increase the Earned Income Tax Credit (EITC), particularly for households without children, for whom it is currently minuscule.[28]

To help households in which no one currently is employed, we should vigorously promote employment of persons who are able to work, provide a decent minimum income for those who aren't, and deal on a case-by-case basis with those who are fit to work but don't. This would require four changes. First, we would need to alter our approach to caseworkers and the assistance they provide. In theory, caseworkers help TANF recipients find jobs, but in reality many are undertrained, overworked, and have limited means to provide real help.[29] We need caseworkers who are well trained, connected to local labor market needs, committed to their job, and not swamped with clients. They must be able to make realistic judgments about when clients can make it in the work force and when the best solution is simply to help them survive.

Second, the government would need to act as an employer of last resort. Sometimes this will help people move up the job ladder, and sometimes it won't. That's okay. We should think of make-work not primarily as a route to "real" employment but rather as an insurance mechanism for those who otherwise would be excluded from the labor market.

Third, in bad economic times, we would need to allow more exemptions to existing limits on access to government assistance programs. For example, during the 2008–09 recession and its aftermath, the five-year lifetime limit for receiving TANF, instituted in the mid-1990s, proved too strict, causing needless hardship and suffering.[30]

Fourth, the benefit amounts would need to be increased and eligibility criteria eased for key social assistance programs—

TANF, general assistance, food stamps, housing assistance, and energy assistance. Given the limit on the duration of receiving TANF, a generous benefit level is no longer much of an impediment to employment.

For the elderly, the challenge of low income is different. Income security in retirement rests on three tiers. The first is personal saving, which has weakened considerably over the past decades. Average household savings as a share of disposable household income fell from 10 percent in the 1970s to 8 percent in the 1980s to 5 percent in the 1990s to 3 percent in the 2000s.[31]

The second is Social Security, which provides benefits to around 90 percent of elderly Americans. Thankfully, this program has been strengthened. Social Security's average benefit level (adjusted for inflation) increased from $10,000 in 1979 to $15,000 today. It's an excellent program, and with a few tweaks it will be solvent and effective for generations to come.[32] But it was never intended to be the sole source of income for retirees. After all, $15,000 isn't much to live on, even if you don't have a mortgage to pay. There is a good case for increasing Social Security benefits.

The third tier is private—usually employer-based—pensions. The share of Americans under age sixty-five who participate in an employer pension plan has remained steady during the past several decades at around 60 percent.[33] But whereas a generation ago most Americans had a defined-benefit plan, now fewer than one-third do. These have been replaced by defined-contribution plans, such as 401(k)s.[34] The problem with defined-contribution plans is that employees and employers tend to not contribute enough to them and to not keep the money in them long enough.[35] A solution is to enhance defined-contribution plans by making contributing the default option and making it available to everyone.[36] In this scenario, employers with an existing plan could continue it, but they would have to automatically enroll all employees and deduct a portion of earnings toward contributions unless an employee elects to opt out. Employers without an existing plan could participate in a new universal retirement fund, and this fund would automatically enroll any employee without an available employer plan. Workers who lack an employer match would be eligible for matching contributions from the government.

What about income instability? Here, four changes would help. One is sickness insurance. The United States is the only rich nation without a public sickness insurance program.[37] Many large private sector firms offer employees some paid sick days, but one in three employed Americans gets zero days of paid sick leave.[38]

A second is paid parental leave. Instead of merely requiring that firms allow three months of unpaid leave, a regulation established by the 1993 Family and Medical Leave Act, we would do well to emulate the Nordic approach. In Sweden, parents of a newborn child have thirteen months of job-protected paid leave, with the benefit level set at approximately 80 percent of earnings. Additionally, parents can take four months off per year to care for a sick child up to age twelve, paid at the same level as parental leave.[39]

Third, only about 40 percent of unemployed Americans qualify for unemployment insurance.[40] We should expand access to this program.[41]

Fourth, we should add a new wage insurance program.[42] Some Americans who get laid off cannot find a new job that pays as well as their former position and are therefore forced to settle for a lower salary. Wage insurance would fill half of the gap between the former pay and the new lower wage for a few years.

Finally, there is the problem of unexpected large expenses. The obvious first step is universal health insurance. We also need to address the inadequacy of some existing health insurance plans. This requires more and clearer information for consumers about available plans, improved affordability of good plans, and probably a government option (such as Medicare) that would be available to all Americans irrespective of age or income. Other rich countries have shown that it's possible to assure high-quality healthcare for all citizens without breaking the bank.[43]

OPPORTUNITY

One of our country's major successes in the last half-century is the progress we've made in reducing obstacles to opportunity stemming from gender and race. When it comes to obstacles related to family background, however, the news is disappointing. Americans growing up in less-advantaged homes have far less opportunity than their counterparts from better-off families, and this opportunity gap hasn't narrowed in recent decades. If anything, it may have widened.

There is no straightforward way to measure opportunity, so social scientists tend to infer from outcomes, such as employment or earnings. If we find that a particular group fares worse than others, we suspect a barrier to opportunity. It isn't ironclad proof, but it's the best we can do. To assess equality of opportunity among people from different family backgrounds, we look at each person's position on the income ladder relative to her or his parents' position (this is called "relative intergenerational mobility").[44]

Opportunity differs significantly by family background.[45] Think of the income distribution as a ladder with five rungs, each representing a fifth of the population. In a society with equal opportunity, every person would have a 20 percent chance of landing on each of the five rungs and hence a 60 percent chance of landing on the middle rung or a higher one. The reality is quite different. An American born into a family in the bottom fifth of incomes between the mid-1960s and the mid-1980s has roughly a 30 percent chance of reaching the middle fifth or higher in adulthood, whereas an American born into the middle fifth has a 66 percent chance of ending up in the middle fifth or higher and one born into the top fifth has an 80 percent chance.[46]

Between the mid-1800s and the 1970s, differences in opportunity based on socioeconomic background decreased.[47] But in the past generation, a number of the key determinants of attainment—such as family structure, parents' income, parenting styles and behaviors, education, employment and earnings, and partner selection—have moved in a direction that is likely to widen the opportunity gap rather than narrow it.

Children who don't grow up with both of their original parents tend to fare worse on a host of outcomes, from school completion to staying out of prison to earning more in adulthood. The collapse of the two-parent family has been most pronounced among parents without a college degree. The same appears to be true of parental instability (e.g., a parent who goes from being married to being single and then becomes partnered or married again), which some experts believe is more consequential for children than the number of parents in the home.[48]

Low-income parents aren't able to spend as much on goods and services aimed at enriching their children, such as music lessons, travel, and summer camp.[49] Inequality in incomes has increased since the 1970s, and during this period we've seen a rise in inequality of families' expenditures on their children.[50]

Parents with less education and income tend to read less to their children and help less with schoolwork. They are less likely to set and enforce clear rules and routines. They are less likely to encourage their children to aspire to high achievement in school and at work. Low-income parents are more likely to be anxious and stressed, which may affect the general home atmosphere and hinder their ability to provide emotional support to their children.[51] With the advent of the modern intensive-parenting culture, these types of differences in parenting styles and traits seem to have increased.[52]

Differences in out-of-home care also have widened. Most preschool-aged children used to stay at home with their mothers, but now many are in out-of-home childcare. While children of affluent parents attend high-quality development-oriented preschools, kids of poorer parents are more likely to be left with a neighborhood babysitter who lets them watch television rather than engaging them in more enriching activities.

Elementary and secondary schools help to equalize opportunity. However, their success in doing so is hampered by continued disparities in school funding.[53]

Children in low-income families are more likely to grow up in neighborhoods with high crime, many unemployed adults, and weak institutions and organizations (e.g., civic groups, churches, and sports leagues). In recent decades, the degree of residential segregation by class has increased. Education and income gaps in participation in schools, civic organizations, churches, and other institutions have widened. And compared to their higher-income peers, children from low-income families have become less and less likely to participate in school-based extracurricular activities, from clubs to marching bands to sports teams.[54]

Partly because they lag behind at the end of high school, and partly because college is so expensive, children from poor backgrounds are less likely than others to enter and complete college. This gap has increased in the past generation.[55]

When it comes to getting a job, the story is no better. Low-income parents tend to have fewer valuable connections to help their children find good positions. Some people from poor homes are further hampered by a lack of English-language skills. Another disadvantage for the lower-income population is that, in the 1970s and 1980s, the United States began incarcerating more young men, often for minor offenses. Having a criminal record makes it more difficult to get a stable job with decent pay.[56] A number of developments, including technological advances, globalization, a loss of manufacturing employment, and the decline of unions, have reduced the number of jobs that require limited skills but pay a middle-class wage—the kind of work that once lifted poorer Americans into the middle class.[57]

Finally, Americans increasingly tend to marry or partner with someone who has attained a similar level of education.[58] This shift toward greater marital homogamy is likely to have further lowered the odds that someone starting at the bottom of the socioeconomic ladder will end up in the middle or higher.

How can we reduce the opportunity gap? There are a host of potentially useful steps. We'll focus on just three. First, America should move toward universal, high-quality, affordable early education. This is another area in which we can learn from the Nordic countries. Danish and Swedish parents can take a paid year off work following the birth of a child. After that, parents can put their child in a public or cooperative early education center. Early education teachers get training and pay comparable to elementary school teachers. Parents pay a fee, but it is capped at around 10 percent of a household's income. In these countries, the influence of parents' education, income, and parenting practices on their children's cognitive abilities, likelihood of completing high school and college, and labor market success is weaker than elsewhere.[59] Evidence increasingly suggests that the early years are the most important ones for developing cognitive and noncognitive skills, so the Nordic countries' success in equalizing opportunity very likely owes partly, perhaps largely, to early education.[60]

The availability of affordable early education also makes it easier for parents, especially mothers, to get back into the workforce, thereby enhancing women's economic opportunities and boosting family incomes.[61] In a country that values employment, this is a service the government should support. About half of preschool-age American children already are in out-of-home care, but much of that care is unregulated and hence of uneven quality.[62] While some parents can pay for excellent childcare, many cannot. Universal early education would change that.

Second, we need to increase college entry and graduation rates among Americans from less-advantaged homes.[63] On average, about two-thirds of a typical cohort enter college and about one-third end up with a four-year degree. But both entry and completion vary starkly by family income. Among those whose parents' income is in the bottom quarter, just 30 percent begin college and just 10 percent get a four-year degree. These percentages are only slightly higher than they were a generation ago.

Better preparation in elementary and secondary school can encourage more low-income children to go to college and enable them to succeed once there. Along the same lines, we need to improve performance and retention among less-advantaged youth who enter college via better instruction, advising, support, and close monitoring.

A more straightforward (and complementary) approach would be to reduce the cost of college.[64] The average cost per year for tuition and room and board at a public four-year university, taking into account grants and financial aid, is about $12,000. For the lower fifth of American households, whose average income is $19,500, that price is a tall order. In Denmark, Finland, Norway, and Sweden, attending a four-year public university is free. In those countries, the odds that a person whose parents didn't complete high school will attend college are between 40 and 60 percent, compared to just 30 percent in the United States.[65]

Third, it would help to put more money into the hands of low-income families with children. A recent study found that, for Americans growing up in the 1970s and 1980s, an increase in family income of a mere $3,000 a year during the first five years of life was associated with nearly 20 percent higher earnings later in life.[66] We should follow the lead of other affluent countries, including those that do better on equality of opportunity, and offer a universal child allowance. Our current version, the Child Tax Credit, gives families a maximum of $1,000 a year per child. And receipt of the money is contingent on filing a federal tax return, which not all low-income families do. In Canada, by contrast, a family with two children receives an annual allowance of around $3,000, and low-income families with two children can receive more than $6,000.[67]

FAIRLY SHARED PROSPERITY

When a country prospers, everyone should prosper. In the period between World War II and the mid-1970s, economic growth was good for all Americans, not just those at the top. The incomes of middle-class and lower-class households rose in lockstep with GDP per capita. Since then, however, the incomes of ordinary Americans have risen very slowly relative to the economy. As the economy has grown, not enough of that growth has reached households in the middle and below.[68]

Ordinary Americans have two principal sources of income: earnings (money from paid work) and net government transfers (government transfers received minus taxes paid). From the 1940s through the 1970s, rising wages were the most important source of income growth for working-age Americans, though employment and net government transfers also increased.[69] Since the late 1970s, the story has been very different.

Wages for Americans at the median and below have been nearly flat since 1979. The institutional configuration that enabled rising wages during the post–World War II years—when many American firms faced limited product market competition, limited pressure from shareholders to maximize short-run profits, and significant pressure from unions (or the threat of unions) to pass on a healthy share of profits to employees—is gone. A host of additional developments now also push against wage growth: technological change, the slow growth of educational attainment, the shift of employment from manufacturing to services, a more general trend away from middle-income jobs, an influx of less-skilled immigrants, the growing prevalence of winner-take-all labor markets, a shift toward pay based on performance, and a fall in the (inflation-adjusted) minimum wage.

Employment is the other potential source of rising earnings. The United States has a set of institutions and policies that in theory should be conducive to rapid employment growth: a low wage floor, limited labor market regulations, relatively stingy government benefits, and comparatively low taxes. During the 1980s and 1990s, the employment rate among twenty-five- to sixty-four-year-olds rose by 7 percentage points, a larger increase than many other rich nations achieved during those two decades.[70] Some commentators took to referring to our economy as the "great American jobs machine."

But then the rose lost its bloom. The early years of recovery after the 2001 recession featured feeble job growth, and things didn't improve much after that. By the peak year, 2007, the employment rate hadn't yet recovered to its 2000 level. During the subsequent economic crash, virtually all of the progress of the 1980s and 1990s was erased.

Government transfers include money from Social Security, unemployment compensation, disability payments, the EITC, food stamps, TANF, and several other programs. As the United States grew richer in the decades following World War II, the benefit levels for many programs were increased. But in recent decades, such increases have been the exception rather than the rule.

So the story since the late 1970s is as follows. Wages in the middle and below have barely budged. Employment has increased, and this has been an important help, but it hasn't done enough. Net government transfers, like wages, have risen only slightly. This is what lies behind the slow income growth for ordinary Americans.

What can we learn from the experiences of other rich countries in recent decades? Most have achieved larger income increases for low-end households than the United States has. That's not mainly because of increases in low-end wages or employment. In almost all affluent nations, the earnings of low-end households have risen little, if at all, since the late 1970s. Instead, it is increases in government transfers that have tended to drive up household incomes.[71]

Most other rich nations have also done better than we have in securing rising incomes for middle-income households.[72] For this group, wages and employment tend to play a more important role than they do for other groups. Many affluent countries have stronger unions and collective bargaining than America does, and that has helped those in the middle class get wage increases. In the 1980s and 1990s, the United States achieved comparatively rapid employment growth, but since then we have fallen behind, perhaps in part because of the limited supports we provide for work-family balance.[73]

How can we get wages rising again? A tight labor market would help. The one encouraging period for wages in the past generation was the late 1990s, and what mainly distinguishes those years from the rest of the past three decades is a low unemployment rate. The current chair of the Federal Reserve, Janet Yellen, is sympathetic to the fact that the Fed's mandate includes not only low inflation but also "full employment" (low unemployment). If the Fed is patient during the next period of strong economic growth, and the resulting tight labor market yields wage increases for lower-earning Americans without contributing to an inflationary spike or an asset bubble, the experience might alter the norm under which the Fed operates going forward. Public pressure could also help shift that norm.

A straightforward way to ensure a rise in wages for at least some in the bottom half would be to increase the statutory federal minimum wage from its current level of $7.25 an hour. More important, the minimum wage should be indexed to inflation. This wouldn't ensure that it keeps up with growth of the economy, but it would at least guarantee that it doesn't lag relative to prices.

What about employment? As of 2014, 84 percent of prime-working-age (ages twenty-five to fifty-four) males, 70 percent of prime-working-age females, and 61 percent of the near-elderly (ages fifty-five to sixty-four) were employed.[74] We may get only a little increase among prime-age men going forward, but among women and the near-elderly there is substantial room for growth.

How can we do it? Adequate demand is essential, but in the absence of a 1990s- or 2000s-style stock market or housing bubble to fuel consumer spending, it isn't clear where the demand will come from. Early education and paid parental leave could boost the employment rate of women. We can do better at making low-end jobs pay well enough to be attractive, via a higher minimum wage and a more generous EITC. Extensive individualized assistance for those who struggle in the labor market would also help.[75] And the government can directly promote job creation by subsidizing private sector job growth and by creating public sector jobs.[76]

Even if we do return to sustained employment growth, there is a limit to how far that can take us in boosting household incomes, because the employment rate has a ceiling. If and when most working-age adults are employed, we won't be able to raise household incomes by adding more jobs. We'll have to rely on wage growth. But what if wages remain stagnant? One useful strategy would be to expand public goods, services, spaces, and mandated free time—such as childcare, health care, roads and bridges, parks, paid parental leave, and paid vacations. This would lift the living standards of households directly and free up some income for purchasing other goods and services.[77]

In addition, we ought to consider a government program that can compensate for stagnant or slowly rising household incomes in a context of robust economic growth.[78] One possibility is to extend the EITC well into the middle class and to tie (index) it to GDP per capita.[79] This would give ordinary households that have at least some earnings a bit of additional money each year, in many instances a few thousand dollars. And over time, it would help to restore the link between growth of the economy and growth of household incomes.[80]

CAN WE PAY FOR IT?

We recommend establishing a host of new public programs and expanding some existing ones:

- Expanded government investment in infrastructure and public spaces
- Universal health care
- One-year paid parental leave
- Universal early education
- Increased public funding of college education
- Equalization of the financing of public K–12 schools
- Increased Child Tax Credit or a new cash allowance for poor families with children
- Sickness insurance
- Eased eligibility criteria for unemployment insurance
- Wage insurance
- Supplemental defined-contribution pension plan with automatic enrollment
- Extensive, personalized support with job searches and (re)training
- Government as employer of last resort
- Minimum wage increased modestly and indexed to prices

- EITC extended further up the income ladder and indexed to average compensation
- Social assistance with a higher benefit level and more support for employment

This won't come cheap. As a rough estimate, we're looking at a rise in government spending in the neighborhood of 10 percent of GDP. Is that beyond the pale? Figure 1.1 puts it in proper perspective. If our government expenditures rise from 38 percent of GDP to around 48 percent, we will be only a little above the current norm among the world's rich nations. Moreover, an increase of 10 percent of GDP would be much smaller than the increase that occurred in the United States between 1920 and today.

How can we pay for this? The politics are difficult, to be sure. But as a technical matter, altering our tax system to raise an additional 10 percent of GDP in government revenue would be simple. Adding a national consumption tax could get us halfway there. And an assortment of relatively minor additions and adjustments to the tax system—such as modestly increasing the effective income tax rate for the top 1 percent of households, adding a carbon tax and a small financial transactions tax, and increasing the earnings threshold for the payroll tax—would take us the rest of the way.[81]

WHAT EXACTLY DO WE MEAN BY "BIGGER GOVERNMENT"?

We're arguing that Americans would benefit from a bigger government. But "bigger" here refers solely to how much of the GDP our government taxes and spends. Government does many other things, and whether or not they should be expanded is a

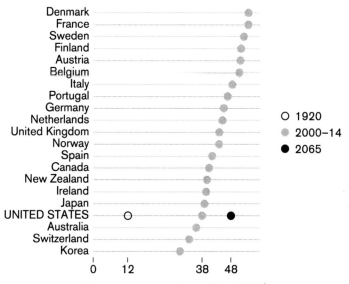

Figure 1.1. Government expenditures as a share of GDP. Includes government at all levels: national, regional, and local. Sources: 2000–2014 averages are from the Organization for Economic Cooperation and Development's National Accounts at a Glance online database. The 12 percent figure for the United States in 1920 is from Tanzi 2011, table 1. The 48 percent figure for the United States in 2065 is our projection.

separate question. Indeed, the country would be better off if the degree of government intervention in some areas were to shrink.

For instance, we allow large pharmaceutical companies to monopolize the provision of certain drugs via patents. Some are drugs these companies invent; others are drugs created by smaller companies whose patents the larger firms buy. Because these drugs relieve pain, enhance pleasure, and prolong life, they are in high demand. The monopoly secured by patents allows pharmaceutical firms to charge extremely high prices for these drugs. One estimate puts the total above-market cost at

$270 billion a year, which is more than we spend on many of our public social programs.[82] Also, the huge monetary benefit conferred by patent protection encourages pharmaceutical firms to give less attention to drugs that, although they may be of considerable medical benefit, won't qualify for patent exclusivity.[83] Weakening patent protection and thereby exposing pharmaceutical providers to greater competition might significantly enhance well-being. We would need to ensure that companies continue to have a strong incentive to invest in research on new drugs, but there are ways to do this that don't rely on lengthy patent protection.[84]

There are other government rules, regulations, and practices that inhibit competition or privilege particular firms and industries. Patent law limits competition not just in the pharmaceuticals market but also in those of computer software, entertainment, and a number of other products.[85] Licensing, credentialing, and certification requirements for occupations or particular types of businesses dampen competition in product markets—from medical care to legal services to education to ground transportation to hairdressing.[86] Zoning restrictions and historic preservation designations limit expansion of housing units in large cities by imposing building height restrictions and preventing new construction on much of the available land.[87] Because the federal government has tended to treat large banks as "too big to fail," investors and management know they are likely to be rescued by taxpayers if their bets go sour, and this allows those banks to engage in riskier strategies that have potentially higher profit margins and encourages investors to choose those banks.[88]

In each of these areas, and surely some others, America would fare better with less government involvement rather than more. But when it comes to infrastructure and social policy, the case for a bigger government is strong.

WILL BIGGER GOVERNMENT HURT THE ECONOMY?

Opposition to increased public social expenditures and higher taxes stems mainly from the claim that they are bad for the economy. High taxes and generous government benefits may reduce the financial incentive to work harder or longer, invest in more skills, and start a new company or expand an existing one. And when government provides goods and services directly, it inevitably wastes some resources. On the other hand, the incentive effect of higher taxes can work in the opposite direction: if tax rates go up, people may work *more* in order to end up with the same after-tax income as they previously had. And some of what the government does helps the economy by boosting capabilities, enhancing mobility, reducing anxiety, and encouraging risk-taking. There surely is a point—a tipping point—beyond which government taxing and spending harms the economy. But where are we in relation to that point? Are we already past it, as some claim? Or are we still well below it?

Theory and studies of individual behavior are helpful in exploring this issue, but the most relevant guidance comes from observing nations. What happens to economic growth when a country increases the generosity of its public social programs? What happens when it raises taxes? Do countries with bigger government grow more slowly? Here we can draw on America's experience and that of other rich nations over the past 150 years. Chapters 2 and 3 do just that.

CHAPTER TWO

Are Government Social Programs Bad for Economic Growth?

PETER LINDERT

Adam Smith wrote his famous defense of the free market in an age when governments were still tiny by today's standards, yet he devoted considerable thought to the proper role of government. Those who cite him as the ultimate champion of small government have overlooked, knowingly or not, much of what he wrote on this topic. They might want to give fresh attention to passages like this one, from the 1766 edition of his *Lectures on Jurisprudence:*

> We may observe that the government in a civilized country is much more expensive than in a barbarous one; and when we say that one government is more expensive than another, it is the same as if we said that the one country is farther advanced in improvement than another. To say that the government is expensive and the people not oppressed is to say that the people are rich. There are many expences necessary in a civilized country for which there is no occasion in one that is barbarous.[1]

In that 1766 lecture, the necessary expenses he had in mind were what we would call infrastructure, both civilian and military.

Within ten years, however, when *Wealth of Nations* was published, he had added a case for tax-funded primary education.[2] His case rested on a basic point echoed in today's economics: if individuals failed to capture all the social gains from providing these services, then individuals could not be relied upon to provide enough of them. In these cases, the government needed to step in:

> [An essential] duty of the sovereign or commonwealth is that of erecting and maintaining those publick institutions and those publick works, which, though they may be in the highest degree advantageous to a great society, are, however, of such a nature that the [social] profit could never repay the expence to any individual or small number of individuals, and which it, therefore, cannot be expected that any individual or small number of individuals should erect or maintain....
>
> When the institutions or publick works which are beneficial to the whole society, either cannot be maintained altogether, or are not maintained altogether by the contribution of such members of the society as are most immediately benefited by them, the deficiency must in most cases be made up by the general contribution of the whole society.[3]

This is not to say that Smith liked taxes and big government for their own sake. On the contrary, he saw waste in much of the government spending of his day, especially in the subsidy to unproductive high offices handed to political favorites. He railed at length against tariffs on imported goods, such as England's infamous Corn Laws. Yet he clearly understood that external benefits could justify tax-based social expenditure.

Remarkably, government expense has risen far above any level that had been experienced in human history up to Smith's lifetime. As he predicted even then, the places with the highest government spending today are exactly those "civilized countries" that are "farther advanced in improvement." In the ensuing centuries, the enormous expansion of government has been dominated by civilian social spending, the kind Smith barely touched on when making his case for tax-based funding of universal primary education. The rising social expenditures are defended as having the same beyond-private benefits as the ones Smith envisioned for "those publick institutions and those publick works." Yet the rise in tax-based social expenditures remains controversial in a world of clashing self-interests. This chapter weighs the evidence regarding their effects on national economic growth.

Since World War II, about a dozen rich countries have channeled more than a fifth of gross domestic product (GDP) into "social transfers," and this figure rises to about a quarter of GDP if we include public education as part of "social spending."[4] Those countries, in order of their social transfer share of GDP in the first decade of this century, are France, Sweden, Austria, Belgium, Denmark, Germany, Finland, Italy, Portugal, and Spain, with Norway, the Netherlands, and the United Kingdom near the margin. Contrasting their experience with that of other countries provides a historical test case for the effects of tax-based social spending. That historical case seems to have delivered these five verdicts:

1. Global history does not show any clear overall negative effect of larger tax-financed social transfers on national product. The widespread belief that a high-budget welfare state would adversely impact a country's GDP is based on theory, not on any appropriate tests. The real world never ran the kinds of experiments that so many have chosen to imagine. The best statistical tests underline a "free lunch puzzle": European nations' large tax-based social budgets have apparently not reduced economic growth.

2. The "free lunch" has taken the form of several fundamental human gains that have been reaped by welfare states. These states have achieved lower income inequality, lower gender inequality, and lower poverty rates, and their citizens have longer lifespans—again, without any clear loss in GDP. What's more, these countries do not suffer any other often-imagined side effects. The large welfare states, particularly in Northern Europe, also have some of the world's cleanest and least corrupt governments, and they have lower budget deficits than the United States, Japan, and other rich countries. And, for what it is worth, public opinion surveys rank their populations as being happier than those of other nations.

3. The free lunch puzzle of the welfare state is easily understood when one examines how actual practice has evolved. Countries on both sides of the Atlantic have made some mistakes when trying to draw an efficient border between governments and markets. The main mistakes on the American side relate to insufficient antipoverty programs, inefficient health insurance, underinvestment in programs to help get mothers back into the workforce, and the undertaxation of addictive goods (tobacco, alcohol, and gasoline).

4. The main institutional mistakes made by Mediterranean European countries relate to excessive protection of vested interests against competition in product and labor markets, not to the social programs of these welfare states. The main causes of crisis since 2007 in Ireland and those Mediterranean countries that are not such comprehensive welfare states have been the real estate bubble and underregulation of finance.

5. One can see two clouds on the horizon for welfare states in the twenty-first century, although neither cloud reveals an economic flaw specific to the welfare state. The first is that the rapid acceleration of population aging poses a serious problem for

financing old age, with public or private funds. Only a few countries have faced this issue so far. The other is the rise of anti-immigrant backlash. This could destroy future public support for universalist social programs, even if those programs remain economically sound.

The remainder of this chapter summarizes the evidence regarding these verdicts.

THE FREE LUNCH PUZZLE
History Shows No Correlations Pitting the Welfare
State—or Progressive Redistribution, or Government
Size—against Growth

For at least three centuries, many conservatives have insisted that tax-funded social spending reduces employment and economic output. So strident is the opposition that one would expect it to have resulted from looking directly at some glaring evidence from history. If the negative effects of welfare state programs are so clear, then perhaps even the raw data should have shown it on a huge IMAX screen.

No such glaring evidence has ever appeared. An obvious starting point would be to glance at the broad sweep of the history of national product, which, if the critics of welfare states are correct, should be lower where tax-based social spending is higher. The glance, however, yields the big-screen evidence shown in figure 2.1. Throughout most of world history, countries have languished in the lower left-hand corner, with widespread poverty and no social help available for the poor, the sick, and the elderly. This is the dreary world that Adam Smith called "barbarous." In the two and a half centuries since Smith wrote, a few dozen countries have taken off into prosperity, as illustrated

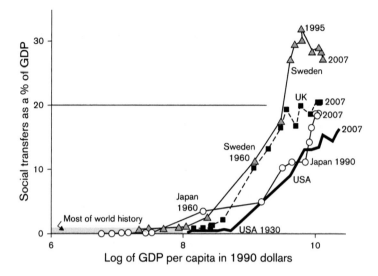

Figure 2.1. The welfare state is young and rich. Sources. The real GDP per capita series up to 2007 is from the Angus Maddison website (www. worldeconomics.com/Data/MadisonHistoricalGDP/Madison%20 Historical%20GDP%20Data.efp). The data for social transfer shares of GDP on the vertical axis for 1880–1930 are from Lindert 1994, and those for 1960–2007 are from the OECD's SOCX series, which is downloadable from OECD iLibrary (www.oecd-ilibrary.org/statistics).

in figure 2.1 by four of Smith's civilized countries—the United Kingdom, the United States, Sweden, and Japan. While prospering, they also channeled an increasingly large share of their national product into taxes that were spent on social programs. Yet they continued to prosper. A person who believes that public social programs weaken initiative and progress might claim reverse causation: perhaps the prosperity bred the wasteful social spending. Yet if the social spending is nothing but a rich country's bad habit, like obesity or recreational drugs, why don't we see any easy evidence of it dragging down GDP per capita?

TABLE 2.1

How social transfers as a share of GDP correlate with growth
and prosperity in nineteen OECD countries, 1880–2007

	Coefficient of correlation between the initial share of social transfers in GDP and	
TIME PERIOD	GROWTH OF GDP/CAPITA	LEVEL OF GDP/CAPITA
1880s	0.10	-0.18
1890s	0.34	-0.05
1900s	-0.23	0.09
1910s	0.12	0.31
1920s	-0.24	0.49
1960s	-0.16	-0.24
1970s	0.34	-0.09
1980s	-0.07	0.09
1990s	-0.11	-0.04
2000s	0.12	-0.19
Simple average of these correlations	0.02	0.02

Sources: Social transfers/GDP for 1880–1930: Welfare, unemployment, pensions, health, and housing subsidies, as given in Lindert (1994, table 1). Social transfers/GDP for 1960–1980: OECD old series (Organization for Economic Cooperation and Development 1985). Social transfers/GDP for 1980–present: OECD new series (Organization for Economic Cooperation and Development 1998). Real GDP per capita: Penn World Table 7.1 (Heston, Summers, and Aten 2012).

Notes: The nineteen countries surveyed are Australia, Austria, Belgium, Canada, Denmark, Finland, France, Germany, Greece (from the 1960s on), Ireland (from the 1960s on), Italy, Japan, the Netherlands, New Zealand, Norway, Sweden, Switzerland, the United Kingdom, and the United States. None of the correlations are statistically significant.

One would rightly demand a closer look than this glance. Sticking to raw correlations for the moment, we may ask whether looking at all countries and over shorter periods of time reveals a negative relationship between their economic growth and their use of welfare state expenditures. Table 2.1 shows the results for as many decades (ten) and as many countries (nineteen) as systematic data is available for. As reported in the table, history again shows no significantly negative relationship between the start-of-decade public social spending share and either the growth or the level of GDP per capita. If we had included the many poorer countries that failed to report their social spending because they had little or none of it, there would be more chance of seeing a positive correlation across history, as figure 2.1 has already hinted at. From all the correlations, we cannot infer a positive causal influence of social spending on economic growth, yet any claim of a negative historical relationship is easy to doubt.

Within nations, as well as between them, we find no secure negative correlation between local governments' social transfers and either the level or growth of national product per capita. If we look at the American states, for instance, for all the conservative media anecdotes about companies fleeing from high-tax states to low-tax ones, there is no net result showing any damage to the higher-taxing and higher-welfare states. The only time the small-government Southern states in the United States rose toward the national average income per capita was in the period 1940–73, when the South reaped disproportionate benefits from government military and aerospace spending. Such spending not only created jobs and income within the South, it also raised Southern pay levels by attracting Southern workers to Northern and Pacific coast cities. Since the rise of welfare payments and other social spending in the 1960s and 1970s, there has been no erosion in the relative incomes of such larger-transfer states as Connecticut and California. There is no indication of massive tax flight, no "race to the bottom."

History Shows No Econometric Evidence
Revealing Net GDP Costs

One should look deeper, if possible, to statistical tests that try to hold other things equal. We know well that both social transfers and national product have many separate, though overlapping, causal determinants. Surely social spending is not just the result of being a rich country, and a country's prosperity depends on much more than just social spending and the incentives it may create.

Since around 1990, economists have poured great effort into developing truly randomized trials, like those now used in medical science. For identifying a causal effect, evidence from these kinds of trials is superior to historical experience, since the randomly selected "treatment" group is subject to influences not experienced by the control group. History is not a randomized trial. It does not offer a treatment group of dozens of societies that were beset by welfare state policies imposed on them by completely outside forces, forces not experienced by a large control group of otherwise similar societies. A few econometric studies have been lucky enough to find "natural experiments" in which history imitates the random-trial laboratory. Yet for large, complex forces like the welfare state, no such randomized historical experiment is available.

Lacking truly random trials, economists are forced to extract what causal insights they can from a messy panel of human experiences over time and space, a panel in which both the determinants of social spending and the determinants of GDP might be disentangled, even though they overlap and are confounded by a host of other forces. I have surveyed the econometric studies available as of a decade ago. None has found a significant negative effect of the whole welfare state package on GDP, at least not any study that has used sound techniques and has made its underlying data available to others.[5] Even the few that announced negative effects but hide their data have failed to show negative effects large enough to imply the major economic damage claimed by some theorists, journalists, and politicians.

The lack of clear negative effects of tax-funded social transfers on the level and growth of GDP is all the more remarkable because the tests typically hobble the welfare state variables with two devices that should produce a negative effect. The first is a handicap that I too have adopted here in order to toughen the test: excluding public spending on education from the welfare state bundle. Public expenditures on education have such clearly positive effects that omitting them raises the odds of finding evidence against the welfare state.[6] The second is that all the tests on historical time-space panels hobble the welfare state with a reverse-causation bias. Safety net programs, such as family assistance or unemployment compensation, are designed so that they pay out more when GDP and jobs slump and less when the economy improves. Thus, unless one somehow perfectly identifies the macroeconomic shocks causing any movement in GDP, transfer spending could appear guilty of causing economic downturns and cutting that spending could then be credited with causing recoveries. This false guilt is analogous to blaming hospitals for causing deaths because so many people die there.[7] Given these two handicaps, it is all the more remarkable that social transfers and other measures of the welfare state do not show clear negative effects on employment or economic growth.

So far, this chapter's presentation of the free lunch result—the absence of a clearly negative effect on GDP—has rested on the fact that social spending as a share of GDP has no clearly negative effect on growth. One might wish for a broader test. Even if the size of social budgets is acquitted of any negative effect, what about two bigger suspects: progressive fiscal redistribution and the overall size of government? Aren't "Robin Hood" and "Leviathan" guilty of dragging down economic growth?

Economists have statistically pursued these other two suspects, yet again without being able to deliver a guilty verdict. As for the measure of progressive redistribution (metaphorically referred to as Robin Hood), international correlations do not show any negative partial correlation with the growth of GDP per capita in the twenty-first century experience. And the overall size of government (Leviathan), measured by its tax take as a share of the national income, cannot be convicted either, as demonstrated in the next chapter of this book. In all cases, we must again acknowledge that the statistical tests are not based on best-practice randomized trials, simply because the history of entire governments—rather than a laboratory experiment—is what we are given. Yet something important can be gleaned even from the complexities of international historical experience, and that real-world history does not convict, or even indict, large government.[8]

Achievements Other Than GDP

While not paying any clear net cost in terms of GDP, the large welfare states have achieved a number of good things with their social transfers[9]:

    1. Their populations have consistently enjoyed a more equal distribution of incomes.[10]

2. They have lower shares of their population in poverty, whether the poverty line is defined as a share of median income or as an absolute level of consumption per person.[11]

3. Their populations tend to have longer life expectancy than those of other OECD countries at similar income levels. (How this might relate to public health care is discussed below.)

4. They have some of the world's cleanest and least corrupt governments, despite what some predicted would happen when large amounts of money pass through government hands.[12]

5. They do not tend to run large budget deficits. There is no correlation at all between the GDP shares of social transfers and the net budget deficit.[13]

6. Finally, international polls of public opinion find high average expressions of personal happiness in the high-spending welfare states.[11]

SOME REASONS WHY

What has made this possible? How could the large welfare states have avoided any clear net cost in terms of GDP while simultaneously making progress on so many social concerns? A balanced tentative answer seems to be that the few ways in which large tax-based social transfer programs reduce GDP are balanced by the ways in which they raise GDP. The heaviest weight on the negative side of the scale seems to be unemployment compensation. Even allowing for some statistical biases against such programs, the empirical literature shows that more generous unemployment compensation does indeed reduce jobs and output somewhat. This negative effect, however, is offset by several GDP-enhancing effects caused by the way in which the welfare state has worked in practice. Let's consider three such effects.

An Efficient Tax and Transfer Mix

While a critic might choose to imagine a foolish hypothetical welfare state riddled with bureaucracy, initiative-discouraging taxes, and transfers that subsidize a lifetime of laziness, no such fiscal system has ever prevailed in a welfare state. On the contrary, real-world welfare states have features that make their tax-based social programs less bureaucratic, less expensive in administrative terms, and less in conflict with economic theory than many have imagined. I will discuss three of them here.

1. *Universalism is efficient on the expenditure side.* One guiding principle is that universalist public transfers and services, those to which everybody is entitled, are cheaper to administer because there is less bureaucratic need to investigate who should be excluded from the benefits.[15]

In the case of health insurance and health care, for example, comparative studies have consistently found that administrative costs are a lower share of health care delivery expenditures in the public programs of Canada and Europe.[16] Universalist public insurance and public provision is less bureaucratic because it does not require spending so many resources on identifying and denying coverage to patients who might prove expensive for one reason or another. Universalist health coverage is also cheaper than means-tested coverage for the poor because it avoids having to investigate the legitimacy of poverty pleas. Similarly, tax-funded public assistance to the poor is cheaper than that provided by private charities due to the latter's administrative expenses for raising donations.[17]

2. *Broader taxes are cheaper to administer.* As countries develop and prosper, they tend to shift toward the broader kinds of taxes that economists consider more efficient. The typical shift is away

from customs duties and other narrow taxes that might greatly disrupt choices (taxes on high-elasticity activities) toward broad taxes on all of a person's income or consumption. Across the first half of the twentieth century, the shift was toward broad income taxation; after that, the shift has been more toward value added taxation (VAT, a flat consumption tax) and sin taxes on addictive products that cause external damages.

The same tax shift affected all prospering countries, whether they became welfare states or not. It was something that happened as government got bigger. Indeed, the tax shift helped them become bigger. Setting aside for the moment the incentive effects of this shift, we merely note here that a broad tax treating everybody, and every source of income, similarly is easier and cheaper to administer. Figure 2.2 shows the dramatic decline in the administrative costs of collecting taxes in Britain since the eighteenth century and in the United States since the nineteenth century. Broader taxation reaps economies of scale to such a degree that today the US Internal Revenue Service spends on administration only half a percent of the amount collected.[18] Welfare states have reaped similar economies of scale as their budgets expanded on the basis of broader forms of taxation.

3. *Large welfare states use a tax mix that, in theory, looks more efficient.* Relative to the smaller-government rich economies, particularly the United States, the large-budget welfare states of Northern Europe get a greater share of their tax revenue from broad consumption taxes and sin taxes on harmful and addictive products such as tobacco, alcohol, and gasoline.[19] The United States, by contrast, gets a greater share of its tax revenue from direct taxes on income and wealth. Conventional economics favors broad sales taxation and sin taxes, and the sin taxes draw added support from those concerned with public health and environmental

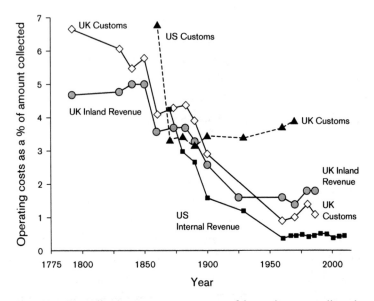

Figure 2.2. Tax collection costs as a percentage of the total amount collected by central government in the United States from 1860 to 2011 and in the United Kingdom from 1787 to 1986. Sources: Data for the administrative cost share of tax collections are from Lindert (2004, vol. 1, ch. 12), and extended data for the United States for the period 1960–2011 are from the IRS Data Book, which can be found at www.irs.gov/uac/Tax-Stats-2. I am indebted to Joel Slemrod for directing me to the updated IRS series.

quality. While we lack reliable econometric evidence that this kind of tax mix is really better for economic growth,[20] conventional economists and economic conservatives *believe* that it is better. Ironically, then, conventional theory favors the kinds of taxation used as a money machine for large welfare states.

More Efficient Health Care

More efficient public health care systems of health insurance and health care provision *may* be responsible for helping people live longer in other countries than in the United States. Three international contrasts involving health insurance and health care delivery provide some circumstantial evidence favoring the performance of countries that have a more universal and publicly funded health system. Two of these three facts are largely unknown to the American general public, while the third has received a great deal of media attention. The first fact, which is generally unappreciated, has already been cited above: America's mixed private-public health insurance has higher bureaucratic administrative costs than a universal, government-funded, single-payer scheme of health insurance (such as the one in place in Canada, for example) or a system dominated by government provision of health services (like those of the United Kingdom and Sweden). The second underappreciated fact is about popular beliefs themselves: while people in all countries have complaints and fears about their health care systems, Americans have for decades had a lower opinion of their system than people surveyed in other countries have of theirs.

The third fact, which has been given more media attention, is that the United States ranks behind other affluent nations in life expectancy. Figure 2.3 restates this contrast for the year 2007, highlighting statistics from the United States, Japan, and some welfare states. The pattern is not a simple one relating to social spending. For example, the world leader in life expectancy is Japan, a country with relatively modest social spending by rich-country standards, although its social spending does tend to tilt toward public health. Still, it is true that people tend to live a bit longer in the average welfare state than in the United States.

As the media have pointed out repeatedly, a significant part of the difference in life expectancy comes in the first year of life, and American babies do not survive as well as those in over a dozen other countries.

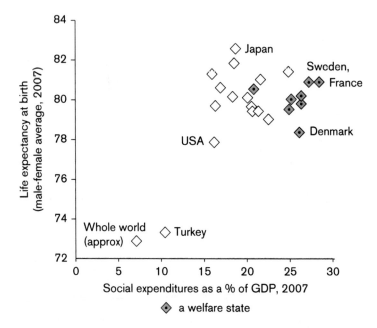

Figure 2.3. Lifespans in welfare states and other countries. Sources: Data on life expectancy around the world is from the United Nations' Demographic Yearbook 2010 and OECD iLibrary (www.oecd-ilibrary.org/statistics). The social transfer share data is from the OECD's SOCX series, which is also downloadable from OECD iLibrary.

Before reviewing the troubled history of American health care, we need to stress two cautionary points about the international contrasts in life expectancy. The first is that these contrasts reflect more than just the performance of the health care system. As far as researchers can tell, the variations in longevity are due more to differences in lifestyle than to differences in health care systems. The slightly shorter lifespan of Americans versus the citizens of other rich countries is due in part to diet. The second is that the international contrasts are not between public and private systems or between large-spending and small-spending countries. Rather, they relate to a peculiarly vexed history of health insurance in the United States, a country that actually spends about as much publicly, and much more privately, on health care than other rich countries.

At the beginning of America's health insurance problems we took a pair of historical wrong turns that left us with too strong a reliance on voluntary employer-based health insurance. The first wrong turn came in the 1940s and 1950s. Employer-based plans gained popularity during World War II, when wage controls prevented employers from competing for scarce workers by offering higher straight pay but allowed them to offer attractive fringe benefits. Then came a tax policy, enacted in 1943 and solidified in a 1954 Supreme Court ruling, that exempted employer contributions to employee health plans from taxation, either as corporate income or as employee income. Thus, one major reform left undone by the Affordable Care Act of 2010 is to remove the special subsidies on employer-based health coverage and to push the industry toward offering plans that are more portable from job to job.[21]

We took our second costly wrong turn in 1965, when the passage of Medicare limited public (aka "socialized") health insurance to those over sixty-five (and those in the military). This wrong turn was caused in part by the first. The passage of Medicare in 1965 was targeted at the elderly because they rightly feared facing costlier health care without jobs to offer them coverage. Some reformers have suggested reducing this elderly bias by extending Medicare to all age groups. In 2010, the Affordable Care Act succeeded in expanding insurance to cover the young, approving extensions of Medicaid and the State Children's Health Insurance Program. It thus made partial steps toward making coverage more universal while proceeding slowly enough to honor (or "grandfather") existing insurance arrangements. Yet one's sixty-fifth birthday still brings a jump in coverage, and moreover, the reduced life expectancy in the United States relative to OECD countries is more significant before the age of sixty-five than after it.[22] The health insurance trap, then, isn't a feature of all countries with small public social programs. It is specific to the United States.

Better Development of Mothers' Human Capital

One of the ways in which the large welfare states gain jobs and productivity is through public policies that invest in career continuity and skills accumulation for mothers. This matters a lot, now that such a large share of women's adulthood is career oriented. Welfare states provide paid parental leaves and public day care with qualified providers. While the underlying reasons are complex and hard to summarize, the policy differences among OECD countries are apparent in their varying fiscal efforts to establish work-life balance for parents, especially mothers, of newborns and infants. Welfare states spend 3 to 4 percent of GDP on supporting work-life balance for new mothers, whereas the United States, Japan, and others spend less than half this share.[23]

Does the extra support for mothers pay off? While it is not easy to estimate gains in productivity from the available microdata, there is at least one aggregate sign of strong benefits: women in countries that provide extra assistance to mothers have market wage rates that are much closer to those of their male counterparts than do women in the United States or Japan, as shown for 1967–2006 in figure 2.4. While it is possible in principle that the higher female/male wage ratio in the Nordic

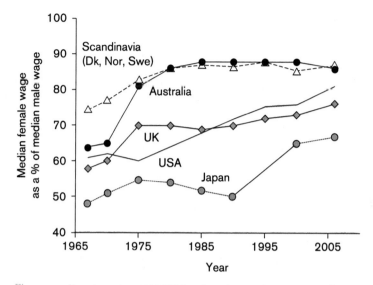

Figure 2.4. Female-male wage ratios in selected countries, 1967–2006. For Denmark, Finland, Norway, and Sweden, figures for 1990 and before are for the manufacturing sector. For Germany, figures prior to 2000 are for West Germany. Data for Germany for 2000 and on are for the manufacturing sector. A new series starts for France, Japan, and Switzerland in 2000. The solid line for Japan indicates a series change between 1990 and 2000. Source: Blau (2012, 372), which cites International Labour Organization, LABORSTA Internet database, http://laborsta.ilo.org.

countries and Australia might reflect forces that lower male earnings, this seems very unlikely. Rather, the differences appear to be in policies that gave mothers the extra human capital that comes from not losing a career when a baby arrives. Indeed, other data show that the wage gap between males and females is specific to policy environments and to marital status: single women are very close to single men in their rates of pay, whereas married women, mostly mothers, are paid less in countries that support them less.

The benefits of real-world government interventions on these welfare-state fronts, combined with the better tax mix of the high-budget welfare states, may help to explain why the statistical evidence has not turned up any negative effect of social transfers on GDP.

WHAT ABOUT THE CRISIS IN PARTS OF EUROPE SINCE 2007?

Since today's high-budget welfare states are European, a common mistake in the media is to attribute the success or failure of any European country to the paradigm of "European welfare state." Thus, when several European economies slumped seriously after the American-led recession that began in 2008, some commentators tied their problems to the welfare state. We should therefore quickly note some ways in which the recession seems to have been quite detached from welfare state spending.

The recession hit Europe after the private real estate market bubble burst loudly in the United States, Ireland, Spain, and Portugal. Nothing about the welfare state caused this. The bursting of the real estate bubble exposed systemic risks that had been building in financial markets since the late 1990s.[24] Underregulated private financial markets crashed first in the United States and Iceland and later in Cyprus. The spread of the recession triggered large deficits in several countries, especially in Mediterranean European countries and the United States. The most prosperous welfare states, such as the Nordic countries and Germany, kept their budgets under control, helped by the fact that their financial sectors had not lunged into the same financial-derivative-based systemic risks taken on by others.

The closest approximation to a link between financial disaster and a welfare state is apparent in the case of Greece. For Greece, the problem is indeed about the public sector, which spent unwisely on pensions and the 2004 Summer Olympics in Athens. However, Greece has never had a true welfare state and, compared to other rich nations, it does little for the poor.

The spread of the recession through Mediterranean countries raises another point that is often missed. There is a separate reason why these countries have such high rates of unemployment. All Mediterranean countries have overprotected their established senior workers with tough antifiring laws since the 1960s. Initially, in the late 1960s and the 1970s, these employee protection laws (EPLs) were intended to prevent unemployment by protecting workers against dismissals, and they may even have induced firms to invest more in the further training of the "insider" workers they were committed to retain. Yet eventually, the firing problem became a hiring problem. Firms became increasingly reluctant to hire new workers who might not prove so productive or whom they would be unable to dismiss in a slump. Over the last quarter of the twentieth century and into this century, the share of "outsiders" in the population who were of labor force age kept rising. More and more of that population lacked the insiders' career experience and their improvements in pay and training. The result was more unemployment and less investment in human productivity. This problem has loomed larger in Mediterranean Europe than in northern Europe, where similar-looking worker rights are modified to allow for more flexibility in job turnover and retraining.[25] The key point is that the defects of EPLs are quite separate from the level of government spending on social programs.

A CLOUD ON THE HORIZON

As previewed earlier in this chapter, social spending faces two clouds on the horizon: a looming pensions trap, and possible backlash against extending social programs to a rising tide of immigrants. The second cloud will not be covered in this chapter, to allow us to focus more clearly on the first cloud.

Mission Drift toward an Elderly Bias

Thus far, the rise of tax-based social insurance and assistance seems like a success story, allowing countries to capture greater income security without incurring a net GDP cost. That success was the result of different kinds of social spending in different countries. Some nations, particularly the United States, achieved the growth effects mainly by offering public education, while European welfare states achieved relatively greater gains by providing improved public health and safety nets for the poor.

Since about the 1960s, however, the further expansion of government social budgets in some of these countries changed focus, drifting away from those human investments that produce the greatest GDP gains and toward investments supporting the elderly and the middle classes, which so far have more neutral effects on GDP. Curiously, this shift has occurred mainly in countries that are *not* welfare states. This section charts the mission shift, first viewing where it occurred, then examining its fingerprints in terms of social expenditure behavior, and finally conjecturing about its efficiency consequences and implications for the future.

Since the 1960s, poverty rates of the elderly have been reduced much more successfully than those of children or per-

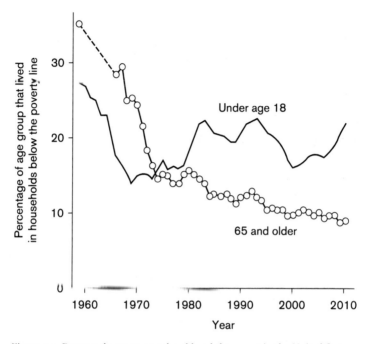

Figure 2.5. Poverty shares among the old and the young in the United States, 1959–2010. Source: census.gov/hhes/www/poverty/data/historical/people. html, accessed December 31, 2011.

sons of working age, according to the averages over groups of OECD countries.[26] In a large number of OECD countries, we see a clear divide in poverty rates around age fifty. All age groups up to fifty years of age experienced an increased poverty share relative to the population as a whole, while those above fifty shifted out of poverty faster than the whole population. Figure 2.5 illustrates this shift in the United States, where poverty declined dramatically for those over sixty-five but not for children.

The drift toward lowering poverty rates more for the elderly than for children and those of working age is clearly tied to a bias in expenditure policy, particularly in certain countries. To show this, one needs to avoid just examining social expenditures as shares of GDP, which can be driven by the age group shares of total population. A more telling kind of expenditure measure is a relative support ratio, which divides social expenditures on the elderly *per elderly person* by social expenditures on the young *per young person*. Such a ratio should be above unity, of course, since the average dependency ratio is higher for those over sixty-five than for those in younger age groups. We can compare the same ratio across countries to detect outliers. Calculating such ratios takes some work, but fortunately much of the work has been done for us already. Figure 2.6 shows some of Julia Lynch's calculations of such an inter-age-group support ratio, graphed against the overall social spending share.[27] The bulk of countries in figure 2.6 have similar inter-age-group ratios, whether they are high-budget welfare states like France and Sweden or lower-budget states like Australia, Ireland, and Canada. There are four outliers, however, all of which have social expenditures that tilt heavily toward the elderly: Japan, the United States, Italy, and Greece. In the case of the United States, one immediately thinks of the fact that Social Security and Medicare, both aimed at providing for Americans over sixty-five, are more generous than public support for the poor of working age. Yet the outliers are not extreme in the generosity of their support for the elderly themselves, as defined by the ratio of social expenditures on the elderly per elderly person divided by GDP per capita. Rather, they stand out because they give so little to those of working age and to children.

Is the relative underinvestment in those under the age of sixty-five something costly in terms of GDP? The answer depends on the social-budget counterfactual one chooses to pose. Here are the two leading candidates:

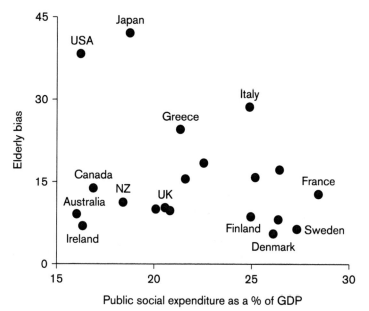

Figure 2.6. Bias toward the elderly in public social spending, 1985–2000. Elderly bias is calculated by dividing the amount of support provided by the government per elderly person by the amount of support per non-elderly person. Source: Lynch 2006. For similar figures covering 1980, 1985, and 1993, see Lynch 2001.

Counterfactual A: Take some of the government money spent on the elderly and shift it toward the leading kinds of social programs for children and those of working age (education, preventive outpatient health care for children, worker retraining, etc.).

Counterfactual B: Privatize pensions, reducing taxes, and mandating individual savings accounts for old age.

Thus far, the text has implied that we are comparing actual practice with counterfactual A, and for this comparison the answer is clearly yes: the bias in favor of the elderly is clearly costly in terms of GDP. That is evident from the simple fact that investing in human development brings an increasingly higher return the earlier the stage of cognitive and career development. The importance of this point has recently been underlined in the writings of Pedro Carneiro and James Heckman, among others, which find that, even among children, the rate of return seems to increase the earlier the child's age at which parents and society intervene.[28]

By contrast, comparison of actual practice with counterfactual B suggests no clear difference in GDP. For all we can tell from twentieth century data, individual saving and tax-financed saving can yield the same GDP result with appropriate adjustments of parameters in programs targeting the elderly. One might note that universal programs like Social Security in the United States are administered with lower bureaucratic costs and lower default risk than private pension plans or individual investments. On the other hand, there is reason to fear that the political process would underfund public pensions. Twentieth century panel data have not allowed us to deny that choosing public pensions over mandated private individual pensions has a zero net effect on GDP.

Thus, the historic drift toward funneling tax money to the elderly either has cost GDP or not, depending on whether one wants to consider counterfactual A or counterfactual B. If there is no clear gain in GDP from shifting social insurance and assistance toward the elderly, why have so many societies done it? The answer seems to be gray power. In the postwar democracies, an ever-greater population share consists of the elderly plus those approaching old age, and the elderly have a relatively high participation rate in politics. They have succeeded in gaining intergenerational transfers, with or without a net effect on GDP.

The Curse of Long Life: Something Has to Give

Yet something has to give in the twenty-first century, as many have long warned. The share of the population consisting of those over the age of sixty-five will go on rising as a share of the adult population, just as it has over recent centuries. The ratios of the elderly to those of working age are rising most ominously in East Asia and Italy, but no country is exempt from this problematic scenario. The main reason is simply the upward march of seniors' life expectancy. The natural solution of having people work to later ages, to hold fixed the share of their adult lives spent at work, has been undermined by a decline in the average age of male retirement, although this has historically contributed less to the increase of years spent in retirement than has the improvement in life expectancy.[29]

Today for every hundred Americans of working age (eighteen to sixty-four years) there are twenty-one elderly Americans (sixty-five years and up), most of them retired. By the year 2050, there will be thirty-six elderly for each hundred Americans of working age, assuming today's rates of birth, migration, and survival hold steady. The balance between people paying into retirement funds and people drawing on them is shifting. We are warned of this in the media every week. In the context of Social Security, 85 percent of economic experts agreed in 2009 with the statement: "The gap between Social Security funds and expenditures will become unsustainably large within the next fifty years if current policies remain unchanged." Actually, the ratio is likely to shift even faster than that because of a newly documented "longevity transition": the life expectancy of seniors is shooting up rapidly, presenting all pension calculations with a possible "curse" of unexpectedly long life.[30] This demographic fact of life has a clear implication for setting pensions: as the share of elderly rises, their annual benefits past the age of sixty-five absolutely cannot rise as fast as the average incomes of those of working age.[31]

This clear warning is both softer and louder than it may sound at first. Softer in the sense that it does not mean pensions have to drop in real purchasing power. Pensions should still keep ahead of the cost of living; they just cannot grow as fast as earned incomes per person of working age, which historically grow at about 1.8 percent a year, adjusting for inflation.

Yet the warning should sound louder when one realizes that it applies to the future of *any* kind of provision for old age, whether private or public. The curse of longer life is not specific to Social Security or other public pensions. The same problem exists even if you rely only on your own savings in old age. To plan ahead, if you live to age sixty-five, you are likely to live to eight-five, even at today's survival rates. Your grandfather, if he reached age sixty-five, only had to plan on living about fourteen years after retirement. Even in such an individual calculation, your annual consumption in retirement has to be a lower share of annual earnings than in the past because you'll live more years. So it's not a problem of government pensions but a problem facing *any* pension plan, be it individual savings, a private job-based pension, or Social Security.

Formulas That Have Worked for Social Security

Fortunately, there are broad formulas that can adjust our pensions to longer lifespans. Here are three formulas that would make Social Security sustainable indefinitely, formulas that private savings plans should also try to emulate.

The first formula is one on which the United States has already done its homework quite well, and it just needs to follow through on. The formula is this: keep the share of adult life spent on Social Security from rising by extending the working age for each benefit rate in proportion to adult life expectancy.

The United States has already taken steps down this path, thanks to the 1983 Greenspan Commission on Social Security Reform. We have advanced the age of "full" retirement benefits from sixty-five to sixty-seven for those born after 1960. The gradual formula adopted in 1983 wisely follows the strategy of grandfathering by not hitting those of middle age with a shock to their life plans.

Yet the news about rising senior longevity means that we must continue to adapt our pension programs. Seniors are increasingly healthy, and the share of them in poverty has declined, so it is not unreasonable for them to receive full Social Security benefits only if they work the same share of their adult lives as their parents. Fixing the share of adult life at work would look something like this: to receive the year 2007's retirement benefit as a percentage of average earnings at any given age, men would need to have worked 51.6 percent of their adult life expectancy, and women would need to have worked 41.5 percent of theirs. This was the case in 2007, and America's progress along this path needs to continue, with more age adjustments.

The second formula builds in an automatic adjustment of the work-retirement balance to the longevity trend, a model that borrows from the "notional defined contribution" pension reform that Sweden set up in the 1990s. The formula is this: as each cohort turns sixty, index their retirement benefits to average life expectancy as measured from age sixty. That is, while every individual's annual pension benefits are still tied to his or her lifetime earnings history, they are indexed to the senior survival odds of everybody in his or her birth cohort. Thus, if you were born in 1980 and you worked from 2000 to 2045, your annual Social Security benefits would be tied to your earnings over those years divided by an index that is tied to life expectancy calculated from survival outcomes for sixty-year-olds around the year 2040. The longer your cohort is expected to live, the lower your annual benefits will be, although of course your benefits are likely to continue for more years. This helps maintain aggregate balance in the pension budget.

The third formula is also patterned after Swedish practice since the 1990s: index annual pension payouts to recent GDP per working-age person.[32] The reasoning behind this is that pensioners' benefits from Social Security should share in the fortunes of the economy. Following this model, when there is a boom, pensioners share in it, by automatic formula. By the same formula, pensions share the pain of a recession as much as others. In the unlikely extreme scenario of another Great Depression, their ultimate safety net would be the same as for the young: public support for the poor plus medical care.

Pre-commitment to such predetermined formulae could remove the pension parameters from the political arena. Of course, while social contracts can make political pre-commitment easier, they cannot guarantee it. Even Sweden softened its preset formula very slightly in response to the 2008–09 slump. Under the original formula, the government was obligated to cut benefits in the years 2010 and 2011. Afraid to follow through on the cuts in 2010, an election year, officials changed the formula to stretch the reductions out over more years. Regardless, the system remains intact, and it still works. In pensions as well as in human investments in health and mothers' careers, welfare state

Sweden stands out as a leader in pursuing rational solutions to social concerns.

CONCLUSION

No welfare state has become poor. There has been no international "race to the bottom," as many skeptics had predicted there would be. Productive people and their wealth have not fled from welfare states any more than productive people prefer a low-tax neighborhood over one with higher taxes but better schools and more public services. In the real world, the welfare state is a Darwinian survivor.

As we have seen, this favorable outcome did not just emerge from a statistical black box. There are plausible reasons for expecting such an outcome, and real-world governments have appreciated that broad safety nets and investing taxpayers' money in human development will raise human productivity. They have financed universal social programs with broad taxes, at low administrative cost, using a mix of taxes that conventional economics would have preferred.

The main challenge is one that is moving toward all developed countries, whether they have large or small government budgets. The aging of the large adult population in OECD countries will put a strain on planning the systems designed to provide benefits for old age, with or without reliance on tax-funded pensions and long-term care. The Nordic welfare states—and, since the 1980s, the United States—have already begun doing their social homework to come up with ways to meet the challenge of an aging population.

In the process, the large-budget welfare states are world leaders in achieving an egalitarian society with lower poverty and less income inequality while maintaining social peace. Perhaps one key to this peaceful egalitarian achievement is the fact that their progressivity was achieved not through friction-causing steeply progressive taxes but through universalism in their social expenditures. In fact, the lower- and middle-income classes that most favored social insurance paid for a good bit of it themselves.

CHAPTER THREE

Would a Bigger Government Hurt the Economy?

JON BAKIJA

If the United States is going to meet the rising costs of promised government retirement benefits and health care for the elderly while doing more to promote economic security, equality of opportunity, and shared prosperity, it will eventually need to increase taxes. Is this the best solution, or should we scale back government and cut taxes, thereby improving incentives for productive economic activity? This is the fundamental political dilemma of our times.

A thoughtful answer ought to depend on many different considerations, but one of the most critical is the long-run economic costs and benefits of larger government and the taxes that go with it. I begin by briefly reviewing some theory that helps to put the debate into perspective. Then I consider evidence on three key empirical questions: How does the long-run economic growth of countries relate to the overall level of taxes and size of government? What is the effect of taxation on peoples' decisions about whether and how much to work? How do taxes affect effort to earn income more generally, especially at the top of the income distribution?

Here is a preview of what the evidence suggests. Among the set of countries comparable to the United States, some have chosen to increase the size of government as a share of GDP much more than others. When looking at data on these countries from the past five or ten decades, there is no convincing evidence that the countries choosing larger government suffered any significant loss of GDP per person as a result. Healthy skepticism is in order regarding claims that growth of government, at least within the range we've seen in countries comparable to the United States, is bad for the economy in the long run.

It is true that *some* econometric studies of cross-country data have found an association between higher taxes and slower economic growth when looking at shorter time frames and controlling for enough other possible influences on economic growth. But even if we take those studies at face value, what they are concluding is that, in the industrialized countries that chose to increase taxes more over time, any negative economic effects of higher taxes seem to have been offset by positive economic effects that are the result of productive government investments (e.g., education, infrastructure) paid for by those taxes and by the more economically efficient public policies that these countries (not coincidentally) tended to choose.

Those studies also raise a number of questions, most notably about whether the associations they find between taxes and growth represent temporarily low taxes during a recession being associated with economies returning to their long-term trends more quickly, or whether permanent changes in taxes are changing the long-run trend of the economy. If we want to know whether making US public policies more like those of Nordic nations would cause significant economic harm in the long run, only the latter is relevant. The longer-run evidence emphasized in this chapter suggests that growth of government probably *hasn't* on balance harmed the long-run trend of real incomes in countries comparable to the United States, even when the tax increases were largely used to finance social transfers.

Tax rates and hours worked are negatively correlated across rich countries, which could reflect the incentive effects of taxes. But this might instead reflect the influence of other policies and institutions that happened to go along with higher taxes, such as legal restrictions on working hours, mandated lengthy vacations, and incentives in government pension systems for early retirement, which are not necessary components of a well-designed welfare state. The best available research—which, if anything, still does too little to address the concerns just noted—suggests that any economic costs of taxes in terms of reduced work are probably modest.

Reductions in top income tax rates are strongly associated with increases in before-tax incomes earned (or reported) by people at the top of the income distribution, both across countries and over time. That *could* reflect a response of productive economic activity to improved incentives caused by tax cuts. If that were the whole explanation, it would imply that progressive taxes (i.e., taxes that are a larger percentage of income for higher-income people) are especially costly in economic terms. But it might instead reflect some combination of other hard-to-measure influences on inequality of pretax incomes that happened to coincide with tax cuts, shifting of reported income from corporate to personal tax returns, or the responses of unproductive but remunerative (i.e., "rent-seeking") activity to tax cuts, none of which would imply that progressive taxes have large economic costs. Across countries, there is no relationship between how much top marginal income tax rates have been cut over the past few decades and the rate of growth in real GDP per person, which lends support to these latter explanations and suggests that the economic cost of highly progressive taxation may not be so large after all.

THE COSTS AND BENEFITS OF TAXATION: A CONCEPTUAL FRAMEWORK

The economic cost of taxation is greater than the amount of tax revenue collected from taxpayers. This is because any tax that is related to a measurable indicator of one's ability to pay taxes, such as income or consumption, reduces the incentive to do economically productive things, and taxpayers change their behavior in response.

For example, suppose someone has the opportunity to earn an extra $1,000 before taxes by doing some additional work, and the leisure that would have to be foregone is only worth $800 to the person. In the absence of taxes, the work gets done. But if there is a 30 percent tax on labor income that reduces the after-tax gain from the work to $700, the person decides it is not worth it to do the extra work. In that case, there's a hidden economic cost of $200—the amount by which the value of the work would have exceeded the value of the foregone leisure. Economists call the $200 cost in this example the "deadweight loss" or the "economic efficiency cost" of the tax.[1]

There are many other ways that people might change their behavior in response to taxation, and these can involve deadweight loss too. Taxes on capital income and corporate profits reduce the incentive to save and invest. Highly progressive taxes take away a particularly large share of the rewards from coming up with a profitable new technology or other innovation, which could in theory reduce the rate of technological advance, a key driver of economic growth. Decisions about schooling and choice of occupation can be distorted by taxes as well. Depending on how tax policy is designed, in some cases it can also negatively influence business decisions about which kinds of investments to undertake, as well as decisions about how much time, effort, and money to put into sheltering one's income from taxes.

Some of these costs could be avoided or mitigated by well-designed tax reform.[2] But if we want a tax system where taxes increase with some measurable indicator of one's ability to pay taxes, it is inevitable that there will be at least some harm to the incentive to do the things that help you get ahead economically. When we design the tax and transfer system to do more to reduce economic inequality, it necessarily weakens those incentives more, resulting in a correspondingly higher economic cost. The size of this economic cost depends on how much people change their behavior in response to the weakened incentives, which is an empirical question. A larger change in behavior corresponds to a larger economic cost.

While taxes impose economic costs, the government spending that those taxes finance produces benefits that can outweigh the costs. The question, then, is how to weigh the benefits against the costs. For example, suppose that for every additional dollar of tax revenue that we collect from affluent taxpayers, we have to make those taxpayers worse off by two dollars, with the difference representing the deadweight loss of the tax. As Arthur Okun memorably put it, taxing the better-off to finance government spending that benefits the worse-off is like carrying water in a leaky bucket, and in this hypothetical example, half the bucket leaks out before reaching its destination.[3]

If we're using the revenue, say, to help pay for high-quality preschool education for kids from disadvantaged families, we might nonetheless decide that the benefits exceed the costs. This might be because we think the gains from spending one more dollar on the education of a disadvantaged child exceed the costs of making an affluent taxpayer worse off by two dollars when the benefits and costs are considered not in dollars but rather in terms of human welfare or happiness, or in terms of promoting justice or equal opportunity.[4] Or it might be because the spending finances an economically sound investment that would not have happened otherwise, in which case even the dollar-valued benefits might eventually exceed the dollar-valued costs.[5] Or it might be some combination of the two.

More generally, the net impact of a change in taxes and government spending on "social welfare" (the aggregate well-being of members of society) can be positive when it promotes "distributive justice" or when it helps to correct a "market failure." Distributive justice is about questions of ethics and philosophy—for example, what is the ethically right policy response to economic inequality that is due to bad luck? Market failure is an economic concept referring to a case where the market fails to do something for which the dollar-valued benefits exceed the dollar-valued costs, in which case we say the market outcome is "economically inefficient." Some market failures arise due to imperfect competition or imperfect information. Another sort of market failure is an externality, which is a case where participants in a market produce benefits for or impose costs on third parties but have no incentive to take those benefits or costs into account. Pollution is a classic example of this. Market failure also arises in the case of public goods, which produce benefits that are non-excludable (meaning people cannot be excluded from benefitting if they don't pay) and non-rival (meaning that when one person benefits from the good, it does not diminish others' ability to benefit from the same unit of the same good). Basic law and order and the resulting reduction in the probability of theft and fraud is a good example of this.[6]

An especially pertinent example of government intervention that could be justified on these grounds is social insurance, which accounted for about 59 percent of US federal government spending in fiscal year 2014.[7] The markets for some important types of insurance are plagued by market failures and also involve important distributive justice concerns.

People value insurance at more than its expected cost because it helps protect them from risk. But if customers know more about their own probability of adverse events than insurance companies do—a problem of imperfect information—then the insurance companies cannot adjust prices to reflect each customer's true expected cost. In that case, some lower-risk customers might no longer find it beneficial to purchase the insurance, resulting in them losing access to a product for which the benefits otherwise would have exceeded the costs. This in turn drives up insurance premiums, which drives even more potential low-risk customers out of the market, pushing up premiums further in a vicious cycle. This is a market failure known as "adverse selection," and the result is economically inefficient. Government could potentially enhance economic efficiency here with government-supplied insurance, or with government mandates and subsidies to individuals to purchase private insurance from a competitive market.

Even in the absence of market failures, unregulated firms in free markets will only insure against events where the good luck or bad luck has not yet been revealed. Thus, those with bad luck in the "lottery of life" in terms of genetics or family background cannot insure against those outcomes in the market. So, for example, should someone who faces high lifetime health care expenses because of genetic bad luck have to bear the full cost of much higher health insurance premiums? This would be economically efficient (as it would reduce adverse selection), but many would also view this as unfair. That's a question of distributive justice. Government could potentially enhance distributive justice in these cases by using taxes and spending to help people to insure themselves against bad luck that the market will not insure against.

The point is that government has both benefits and costs. Some of those benefits and costs will be reflected in economic statistics, and some will not.

We can infer something about the economic costs of taxation by looking at how the level of taxes or government spending correlates with observable economic indicators such as gross domestic product (GDP) or hours worked. GDP is a measure of the total market value of goods and services produced in a country in a given year. It is also a measure of the nation's income, since all production that is sold leads to corresponding income for someone. But even if we were confident that we had identified the causal effect of taxes on GDP, which is challenging enough, we would still have to be careful when interpreting this evidence. For instance, if taxes cause a reduction in hours worked and that in turn causes a decline in GDP, it does suggest there is some deadweight cost from taxation. But the decline in GDP overstates that cost because it does not account for the value of the increased leisure that occurs as a result.

Similarly, some of the benefits of government spending might show up in GDP, but many do not. For example, if government does a good job of addressing market failures that would otherwise lead to underinvestment in education, infrastructure, and scientific research, that can lead to higher measured GDP. Government provision of social insurance might make people more willing to take the risks associated with entrepreneurship and innovation, leading to faster technological progress—that would show up in GDP too.[8] But some benefits of government policy, such as the intrinsic value of greater security, distributive justice, and equality of opportunity or the benefits of a cleaner environment are not reflected in economic statistics such as GDP.

There is an enormous amount of empirical literature in economics documenting evidence of benefits and costs of government interventions that don't show up in GDP, but that is beyond the scope of this chapter. The relevant point here is that, even if the empirical evidence reviewed below were to establish that big government and the taxes that go with it have costs in terms of reducing GDP or hours worked, it would not be sufficient to establish that the costs outweigh the benefits. This is important to keep in mind as we consider the evidence.

CROSS-COUNTRY EVIDENCE ON THE
RELATIONSHIP BETWEEN ECONOMIC
PROSPERITY AND THE OVERALL LEVEL
OF TAXES AND GOVERNMENT SPENDING

A first strategy for inferring the net economic effect of taxation and government spending is to look at how the overall level of taxes or government spending correlates with the level and growth of real GDP per person (i.e., GDP adjusted for inflation and divided by population). As a measure of the well-being of societies, real GDP per person is subject to both the caveats noted earlier and others, but it does have the distinct advantage that it has been measured on a comparable basis for a large number of countries over a long period of time.[9]

My measures of the size of government will be tax revenues and government spending as a percentage of GDP. These are at best rather crude indicators of the role of government in the economy and how that affects incentives. Two countries could be identical along those dimensions, but one might distort incentives much more than the other because, for example, its tax system is riddled with special subsidies, deductions, and loopholes that require higher marginal tax rates. But unlike more refined measures, data for tax revenue and government spending as percentages of GDP are available on a consistently measured basis for many countries over long periods of time. If we wish to identify the *long-run* economic effects of taxes and government spending, that is critical.

Comparison across Countries at a Given Point in Time

Figure 3.1 illustrates what Joel Slemrod has called "an embarrassing fact for those who maintain that high, and highly progressive, taxes are seriously detrimental to a country's prosperity": across all countries in the world for which data are available, there is a strong *positive* correlation between taxes as a share of GDP and real GDP per person.[10] The figure shows, for 182 countries, the relationship between tax revenue as a percentage of GDP and real GDP per person (measured in thousands of 2011 US dollars and adjusted for purchasing power parity) on average during the years 2002 to 2011.

Where possible, I use data on tax revenue raised by general government—that is, the national central government plus any subnational governments such as state, provincial, or local; 110 countries fell into this category, represented by the black dots. In the case of the other 72 countries, represented by the white dots, data are available only for central government tax revenue, so that is what I use. Almost all of the latter are low-income countries, and for the low-income countries where data on subnational government are available, the subnational governments account for only a tiny fraction of general government tax revenue.[11] So, for most of these countries, the white dots should be pretty good indicators of the overall size of government. Nonetheless, just to be safe, when summarizing the average relationship between taxes and GDP per person, I will focus on the black dots.

The upward-sloping grey line in figure 3.1 is the regression line that best fits the cloud of black dots, in a sense summarizing the average relationship between general government tax revenue as a percentage of GDP and real GDP per person. It suggests that, on average, each additional one percent of GDP collected in taxes is associated with $519 dollars of additional income per person, and the relationship is statistically significant (meaning it is unlikely to be due to pure chance).

The vast majority of countries fit the pattern closely: high-income OECD countries, with high taxes and high per capita income, are clustered in the upper right-hand portion of the graph, while large numbers of low-income countries, with low tax revenues relative to GDP and low per capita income, tend to be clustered in the lower left-hand portion of the graph. A similar positive correlation persists within the subgroups of rich and poor countries.[12] A small number of countries, in the upper-left-hand portion of the graph, are inconsistent with this pattern, but all are countries, such as Qatar, that raise large amounts of non-tax revenue through natural resource wealth, particularly oil, meaning that the small levels of tax revenue greatly understate the overall size of their governments.

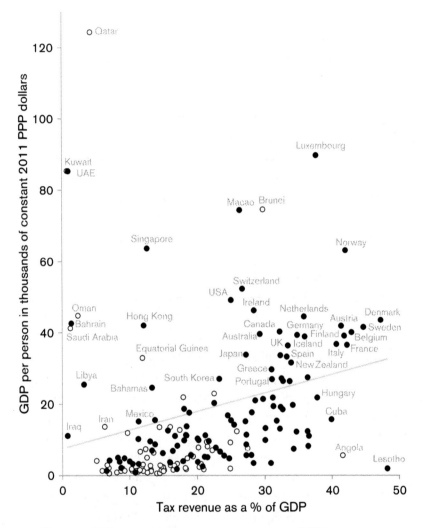

Figure 3.1. GDP per person versus taxes as a percentage of GDP, 2002–2011 averages. GDP per person is given in thousands of constant year 2011 US dollars and is adjusted for purchasing power parity (PPP). Black dots are countries for which general government data are available, and white dots are countries for which only central government data are available. The 2002–2011 averages for a given country are computed using only data from years when both variables are available for that country. Sources: World Bank 2015; International Centre for Tax and Development 2015.

As Slemrod and others who have studied this question are quick to point out, we shouldn't necessarily conclude, based simply on a cross-sectional relationship like that depicted in figure 3.1, that there is no negative causal effect of taxes on GDP per person. Many other factors that are also correlated with GDP per person influence the level of tax revenue as a percentage of GDP. For one thing, higher-income countries clearly have much better administrative capacity to collect taxes and fight tax evasion.[13] So it is possible that taxes have a negative causal effect on GDP per person but that this is obscured in figure 3.1 by the fact that rich countries are the only ones capable of collecting large amounts of tax revenue.

In addition, the causality underlying the positive association in figure 3.1 probably runs in both directions. In particular, higher incomes may cause citizens of a country to demand a larger government. This idea is commonly known as Wagner's law,[14] and there is a large cross-country empirical literature attempting to estimate the causal effect of income on demand for government.[15] It's conceivable that there is a negative causal effect of government size on income (through incentives) but that it is dominated by the positive causal effect of income on government size (through demand for government), with the net result of the bidirectional relationship being the positive correlation we see in figure 3.1.

Advantages of Comparing Relative Changes over Time across Countries, and Cautions

Given the problems involved in trying to infer the causal effects of taxes on GDP from evidence like that in figure 3.1, economists have tended to focus instead on "panel" data, which follow multiple high-income countries over reasonably long periods of time.[16] Using such data, they estimate whether affluent countries that increased taxes and government expenditure by more over time experienced lower economic growth.

Focusing on comparisons of relative changes over time in government size and GDP across countries helps to control for unobservable country differences that are persistent over time. For example, characteristics such as trust and social cohesion might influence both demand for government and level of income, contributing to the positive association shown in figure 3.1. But, to the extent that these characteristics are fairly stable over time, they probably cannot explain why some countries experienced larger increases in the size of government or faster economic growth than others during particular time periods.

Evidence based on relative changes over time also helps to control for influences on growth that are changing in similar ways over time across the set of countries included in the analysis. For instance, the advance of technological knowledge is an important driver of economic growth, but economic researchers lack a good summary measure of technological knowledge. To the extent that the set of countries included in the study have access to similar technological knowledge at each point in time covered in the study, differing trends in technological knowledge would not be able to explain why countries that experienced relatively larger increases in the size of government over a particular time period had better or worse economic growth than similar countries that did not. Limiting comparisons to countries that were at fairly similar levels of economic development at the beginning of the time period studied makes it more likely that the analysis will work well, and it also mitigates the confounding effects of other factors, such as administrative capacity to collect taxes.

Despite these advantages, questions remain about whether such an approach identifies the true effect of government and taxation on economic growth. For example, when some countries experience faster economic growth than similar countries for reasons unrelated to taxes, there still might be reverse causality where the faster rise in income causes a faster rise in the demand for government. An unverifiable hope in this kind of research is that, among the group of countries that have been industrialized for a long time, changes in the size of government relative to GDP were largely driven by the voting public, whose changing tastes—unrelated to income—led them to want more government, rather than by a mechanical effect of rising incomes on demand for government. Moreover, it is sometimes argued that any reverse causality induced by Wagner's law would tend to bias our estimated effect of taxes on the level or growth of income away from the hypothesized negative effect so that our estimates would be a conservative test of the hypothesis that high taxes are harmful to economic prosperity.

A study that examines a set of countries that all have high incomes today, but which started the time period under study at very different levels of economic development, is particularly suspect. In that case, we have to worry that the selection of the sample itself might influence the conclusions in a misleading direction. To understand why, consider the example of the small handful of countries, such as Singapore and South Korea, that have transformed from very low-income developing countries back in the early 1960s to high-income developed countries today.[17] It is true that countries such as Singapore and South Korea experienced excellent economic growth since the 1960s and have small governments as a percentage of GDP compared to other high-income countries today. But including them in a panel analysis of the effects of taxes on economic growth while omitting all the other countries that had low incomes back in the 1960s could misleadingly attribute the success of the included countries to their small governments. Figure 3.1 makes clear that there were enormous numbers of other poor countries in the 1960s with small governments that did not experience fast economic growth (as evidenced by their low incomes today). Small governments are *not* what distinguished the fast-growing East Asian "tiger" countries from other low-income countries that did not grow.[18]

It's also true that countries that experienced rapid industrialization since the 1960s, such as the East Asian tigers (Hong Kong, Singapore, South Korea, and Taiwan), did typically follow market-friendly policies in some regards. But their stories are hardly examples of doctrinaire free market orthodoxy. Many of these countries had governments that were quite interventionist in ways that don't show up in tax revenue or government expenditure statistics, such as engaging in extensive industrial policy, relying heavily on state-owned enterprises, redistributing land ownership to reduce inequality, requiring their citizens to save large shares of their income in quasi-public pension schemes, and more.[19]

Another issue is that the process of transforming from a poor country to a rich country is likely to be very different than the process of achieving continued economic growth once a country is already rich, so it is not so clear we can learn much from the former that applies to the latter. Furthermore, one needs data following the same countries over very long period of time to infer the long-run effects of big government, and such data are only available for the small number of countries that industrialized long ago. For these reasons, it makes sense to focus on a smaller set of countries that have had high incomes for a long time and therefore are more comparable to the United States.

Cross-Country Comparisons of Changes in the Size of Government and Economic Growth over the Very Long Run

Figures 3.2a and 3.2b depict how the natural logarithm of real GDP per person (the solid black line) and general government expenditure as a percentage of GDP (the dotted gray line) each evolved between 1870 and 2013 for twelve industrialized nations for which data are available on a reasonably consistent basis going back to the late 1800s or early 1900s.[20] It is useful to express real GDP per person in logarithmic form because then the slope of the line represents the annual growth rate. If a country were to experience a constant annual growth rate over the whole period, its log real GDP per person would be a perfectly straight upward-sloping line. The dashed black line in each graph in figures 3.2a and 3.2b depicts the trend in log real GDP per person for each country from 1870 through 1929, and the forecast of log real GDP per person for each country for subsequent years through 2013 based on the pre–Great Depression trends.[21]

The country time-series graphs in figures 3.2a and 3.2b illustrate some other facts that don't fit the hypothesis that big government has adverse effects on long-term economic growth. Aside from the obvious fact that there is a positive correlation over time between the size of government and the level of real GDP per person (which might be explained away by Wagner's law and improved administrative capacity to collect taxes), there

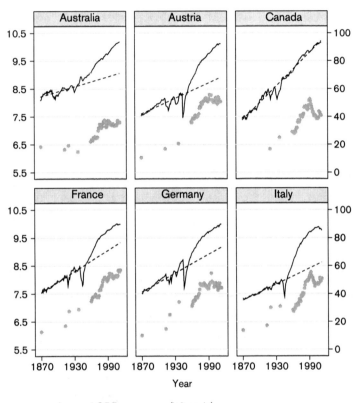

Log real GDP per person (left scale)
Trend in log real GDP per person 1870–1929 (left scale)
General government expenditure % of GDP (right scale)

Figures 3.2a *(this page)* and 3.2b *(opposite)*. Log real GDP per person and general government expenditure as a percentage of GDP in industrialized nations, 1870–2013. Real GDP per person is in constant 1990 US dollars and is adjusted for purchasing power parity. Sources: Maddison Project 2013; World Bank 2015; Tanzi 2011; Organization for Economic Cooperation and Development 1982, 1992, 2000, 2015e; US Bureau of Economic Analysis 2015.

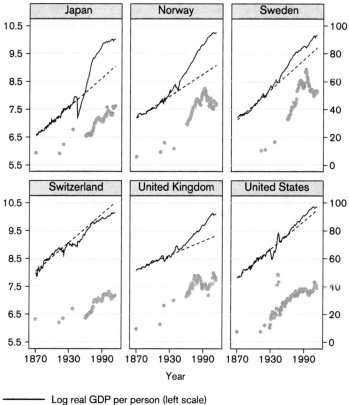

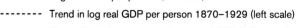

Log real GDP per person (left scale)

Trend in log real GDP per person 1870–1929 (left scale)

General government expenditure % of GDP (right scale)

is also the fact that, among the major industrialized countries of the world for which we have consistent data going far back in time, government expenditure was a much larger percentage of GDP in the second half of the 1870–2013 period than it was in the first half, yet there is no evidence of a slowdown in the long-run economic growth rate in the era of big government.

If anything, the countries with the largest increases in the size of government over time tended to be the ones where the log of real GDP per person experienced a persistent *increase* above the previous long-term historical trend. For example, for the United States, Canada, and Switzerland, the 1870 to 1929 trend in log real GDP per person predicts its subsequent levels through 2013 almost perfectly, despite the fact that government grew dramatically and permanently as a share of GDP in these countries around the time of World War II.[22] The other countries shown in figures 3.2a and 3.2b tended to have larger increases in the size of government than those three, and their log real GDPs per person actually rose significantly *above* their pre-Depression trends in the later era of big government.

We should not necessarily attribute the increase above the trends to beneficial effects of larger increases in government, since the countries with larger increases in the size of government also tended to be ones that started out the poorest. These countries experienced a temporary period of rapid catch-up growth after World War II as they converged toward the income and technology of the United States and restored the capital that was destroyed during the war.[23] Nonetheless, the fact that long-run economic growth in the advanced industrialized nations has been so remarkably stable since the late 1800s despite huge increases in the role of government is striking and inconsistent with the notion that big government is bad for the economy.

In an important 1995 article, Charles I. Jones demonstrated that, for the major industrialized nations of the world, we can reject, with a high degree of statistical confidence, the hypothesis that there have been any *permanent* changes in the growth rate of real GDP per person at all since the late 1800s. Appreciating the significance of this insight and its implications requires a bit of a detour into time-series econometrics jargon.

Technically, Jones demonstrated with formal statistical tests that we could reject the hypothesis that the economic growth rate since the late 1800s was "non-stationary" for each of many advanced industrial nations. A variable is non-stationary if it experiences permanent changes—that is, when the variable increases in a particular period, it is no more likely to go up than to go down in future periods, so changes to the variable tend to persist. By contrast, a variable is "stationary" if it is mean-reverting. In other words, if a stationary variable increases in a certain period, then it is more likely to go down than to go up in future periods, and in the long run it eventually reverts to a stable mean that does not change over time.[24] Jones's evidence suggested that economic growth rates in rich countries since the late 1800s have been stationary. Consistent with what the graphs in figures 3.2a and 3.2b show, log real GDP per person might rise above or fall below its long-run historical trend in a permanent way, but the evidence rejected the notion that there are any permanent changes in the *slope* of log real GDP per person over time (i.e., in the growth rate), at least for the industrialized nations since the late 1800s.[25]

By contrast, visual inspection of figures 3.2a and 3.2b suggests that government expenditure as a percentage of GDP during the period 1870–2013 is non-stationary. In all of these countries, the government expenditure share of GDP experienced a very large and apparently permanent increase over time, with no prospect of being fully reversed.[26] This poses a serious problem for those who believe an increase in government spending and taxes will have a permanent negative effect on the rate of economic growth and more generally to "endogenous growth" models that posit that changes in policy variables can have permanent impacts on growth rates by causing changes in the rate of technological progress.[27]

Responding to the evidence that economic growth rate is stationary while many policy variables that supposedly have persistent effects on the rate of economic growth are non-stationary, Jones noted: "Two possibilities are suggested: either by some astonishing coincidence all of the movements in variables that can have permanent effects on growth rates have been offsetting, or the hallmark of the endogenous growth models, that permanent changes in policy variables have permanent effects on growth rates, is misleading." As a result, the idea that the net effect of big government is to permanently damage the rate of economic growth probably does not make much sense.[28]

The notion that permanent tax increases can't have permanent negative effects on the growth rate narrows the range of possible impacts of taxes and government spending on the economy considerably, but it still leaves room for taxes and government spending to have long-run effects on the *level* of GDP per person. For example, a permanent increase in government's share of GDP could, in principle, cause GDP per person to permanently dip below its historical long-run trend. But figures 3.2a and 3.2b seem to suggest the opposite has occurred over the long run in most rich countries.

To illustrate more clearly whether countries that chose larger increases in government over time experienced any penalty in economic growth over the very long run, figures 3.3a and 3.3b show how the average annual rate of growth in real GDP per person in thirteen countries (the twelve countries in figures 3.2a and 3.2b plus Ireland) between 1913 and 2013 relates to the change in general government expenditure as a percentage of GDP over that same time span.[29]

Even if changes in government spending do not have permanent effects on the long-run growth rate, such changes could, in theory, cause GDP per person to permanently dip below its previous long-run trend, and that would show up as a reduced average annual growth rate when measured over the span of one hundred years. Figure 3.3a shows that, although all of the thirteen countries increased the size of their governments significantly over the past century, there was also enormous variation in how much they increased them, ranging from an 18.5 percent of GDP increase in Australia to a 44 percent of GDP increase in Sweden. Given these magnitudes, if government has an adverse effect on economic growth, the odds are good that we'd be able to detect it here.

Figure 3.3a shows that there is a weak *positive* correlation between the size of the increase in government spending and the long-run growth rate. The estimated regression line, representing the straight line that best fits the dots on the scatterplot, suggests that an increase in government spending of 10 percent of GDP is associated with a 0.2 percentage point *increase* in the annual growth rate, on average, over one hundred years. The relationship, however, is not statistically significant. This means, roughly speaking, that the points on the scatter plot are so randomly scattered that we can't have much confidence that there is a real relationship there.[30]

A potential confounding factor arises because economic theory suggests that countries starting at lower levels of GDP per

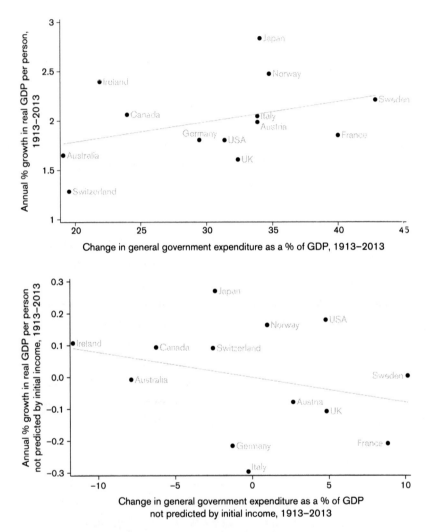

Figures 3.3a *(top)* and 3.3b *(bottom)*. Growth in real GDP per person versus change in government expenditure as a percentage of GDP in industrialized nations, 1913–2013. Real GDP per person is given in constant 1990 US dollars and is adjusted for purchasing power parity. Data for Ireland and Canada are for 1920–2013. Sources: Maddison Project 2013; World Bank 2015; Tanzi 2011; Organization for Economic Cooperation and Development 2015e; US Bureau of Economic Analysis 2015.

person might find it easier to grow quickly. One reason is that poorer countries tend to have lower levels of physical capital (productive machinery, equipment, factories, buildings, and tools) per worker, so additional accumulation of physical capital will tend to have a higher payoff than it will for richer countries, due to the principle of diminishing returns. Another reason is that the richest countries need to innovate and come up with new technologies in order to grow, which is difficult, whereas poorer countries can still achieve a lot of growth by simply copying and applying the technology of the richer countries, which might be easier.

This implies that we ought to expect some convergence in income levels across countries in the long run, as poorer countries experience temporary periods of accelerated growth as they catch up to the leaders." A concern with figure 3.3a is that the countries that started off poorer (relative to other countries at the time) might have subsequently grown faster due to this convergence (or catch-up-growth) just described. This could obscure any negative effects of taxes on growth if starting out relatively poorer was also positively correlated with the subsequent growth in the size of government. Countries that started out poorer did tend to begin with smaller governments because of both weaker administrative capacity to collect taxes and less demand for government (Wagner's law). In that case, we might expect size of government to converge too as the poorer countries catch up to the richer ones in terms of administrative capability and demand for government.

To help control for this, figure 3.3b shows the same relationship as in figure 3.3a, except that it controls for the initial level of GDP per person in 1913. Formally, the way it does this is by estimating a regression of growth against initial income and a regression of change in government size against initial income and then plotting the portions of growth and change in government size that are not predicted by initial income against each other.[*] The slope of the regression line through the scatterplot in figure 3.3b is the association between change in government and growth, holding initial income constant.

In figure 3.3b, the regression line that best fits the data is now downward sloping (suggesting larger increases government are associated with slower income growth), but the implied effect of government on growth is both statistically insignificant and tiny (as suggested by the loose scattering of the dots and the very small scale of the vertical axis). The slope of the regression line suggests that increasing government spending by an additional 10 percent of GDP is associated with a reduction in the average annual growth rate over one hundred years of just 0.08 percentage points per year. The 95 percent confidence interval ranges from -0.26 percentage points to +0.10 percentage points.

Small differences in annual growth rates can have significant consequences over a hundred years, but the point estimate here suggests that a country that otherwise would have the average annual growth rate for the sample (about 2 percent per year) would be only 7 percent poorer after one hundred years if it increased government spending by an extra 10 percent of GDP during that period than if it had not done so.[33]

Given the statistical uncertainty, which is reflected in how seemingly randomly the dots in the scatterplot are scattered and exacerbated by the fact that we have only thirteen data points, we shouldn't draw conclusions from this too confidently. But these thirteen countries accounted for about half of the world's GDP in 1913 (and over a third today), and the data follow them over a hundred years yet reveal no significant association between increase in size of government and economic growth, despite enormous differences in the magnitude of changes in the size of government. That should give us at least a bit of confidence that the economic harm from bigger government is not necessarily large.[34]

The 95 percent confidence interval, which appropriately takes into account the uncertainty arising from the small sample size, rules out the effects of a 10 percent of GDP increase in government spending on economic growth that are more negative than -0.26 percentage points per year and cannot rule out zero or positive effects. So our best guess based on these data is that, among the countries in the sample that chose to increase the size of their governments most dramatically over the past century, the long-run economic cost of doing so, if any, was probably at most very small.

Cross-Country Comparisons of Changes in the Size of Government and Economic Growth since the Early 1960s

If we shift our focus to the period since the early 1960s and switch to using general government tax revenue as a percentage of GDP as our indicator of government size, the available data enable us to expand the analysis to a larger number of countries. Figures 3.4a and 3.4b depict, for each of eighteen industrialized nations, how general government tax revenue as a percentage of GDP and log real GDP per person evolved between the early 1960s and 2013 and how the values of both of these variables compares to those for the United States.[35] In each graph, log real GDP per person for the country in question is shown as a black solid line, while tax as a percentage of GDP is shown as a solid black line with black dots running along it. US log real GDP per person is shown as a dashed line, and US tax as a percentage of GDP is shown as a gray solid line with gray dots.

These graphs make it clearer when the size of government diverged most dramatically across countries. Countries such as Belgium, Denmark, Finland, France, Italy, Netherlands, Norway, and Sweden all had taxes as a percentage of GDP that were pretty close to US levels in the early 1960s, but all of them subsequently increased taxes by around 10 to 15 percent of GDP while the United States held taxes as a percentage of GDP comparatively steady over this period. Much of that divergence occurred during the 1960s and 1970s. Despite this, there is no discernable tendency for the countries that increased taxes more to experience slower economic growth.

Cases where the trajectories of log real GDP per person are particularly steep (meaning growth is especially high) seem associated mostly with countries that started out poorer compared to other countries at the time, which is consistent with the convergence story mentioned earlier. Those countries whose GDP per person started out relatively close to the US level in 1960 had subsequent paths of GDP per person that roughly paralleled that of the United States, regardless of how much taxes increased. Countries such as Denmark, Finland, and Sweden now have much higher tax rates than the United States and do have slightly lower incomes per person than the United States does today, but that small gap in incomes per person was already there in 1960, when the taxes of these countries were not a significantly larger percentage of GDP than in the United States, and the gap in incomes has not widened significantly since then.

Figure 3.5a shows, for twenty-three industrialized countries (adding Greece, Luxembourg, Portugal, and Turkey to the set of countries in figures 3.4a and 3.4b), that countries that had larger increases in tax revenue as a percentage of GDP between the early 1960s and 2013 actually had higher rates of growth of real GDP per person on average. Figure 3.5b shows the same relationship, controlling for the initial level of real GDP per person and the 2013 unemployment rate. Unemployment is a potentially important confounder, as some countries such as Spain and Greece were, as of 2013, still operating well below capacity due to a massive recession that had little or nothing to do with taxes and consequently were suffering unemployment rates well above 20 percent. Once again, the correlation between the change in taxes and the economic growth rate is weakly positive, the opposite of what we would expect if big government had a deleterious long-run effect on the economy.[36]

Econometric Evidence on the Effects of Taxes on Economic Growth

While graphs of the sort presented above are informative, they alone cannot be decisive. They don't do much to control for other factors that might influence economic growth, and they fail to make full use of available information on how the timing of changes in taxation or government spending relates to the timing of changes in the economy. More formal econometric (regression) analysis has the potential to do a better job of this.

There is now a very large body of research that uses multiple regression techniques to estimate the effects of the overall level of taxes and/or government spending on economic growth. Many reviews of this literature express considerable skepticism about whether any of the research has managed to convincingly identify a significant negative causal effect of the overall level of

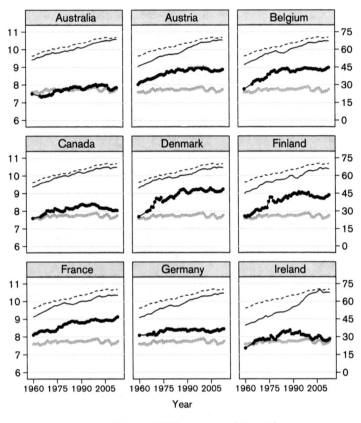

--- US log real GDP per person (left scale)

— Log real GDP per person (left scale)

US tax % of GDP (right scale)

Tax % of GDP (right scale)

Figures 3.4a *(this page)* and 3.4b *(opposite)*. Log real GDP per person and general government tax revenue as a percentage of GDP of rich nations compared to the United States, 1960–2013. Real GDP per person is given in constant 2005 US dollars adjusted for purchasing power parity. Sources: Penn World Tables Version 8.0 (Feenstra, Inklaar, and Timmer 2015); World Bank 2015; Tanzi 2011; Organization for Economic Cooperation and Development 2015a, 2015e.

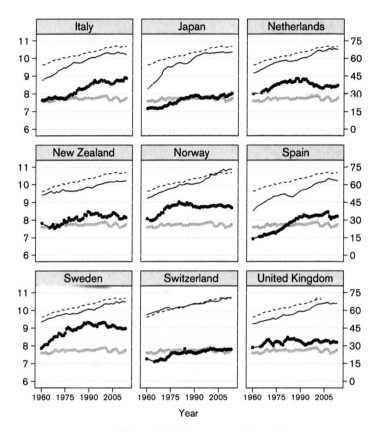

US log real GDP per person (left scale)

Log real GDP per person (left scale)

US tax % of GDP (right scale)

Tax % of GDP (right scale)

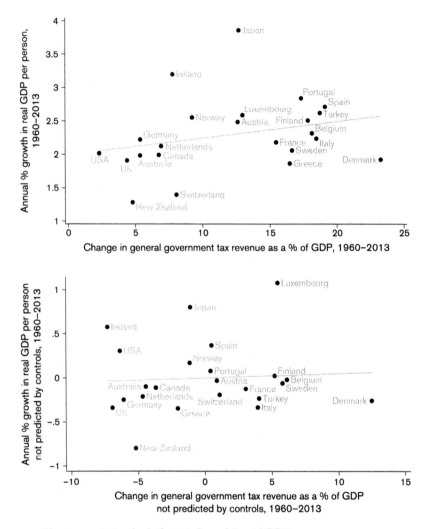

Figures 3.5a *(top)* and 3.5b *(bottom).* Growth in real GDP per person versus change in general government tax revenue as a percentage of GDP, 1960–2013. Data for Greece, Luxembourg, and Turkey are for 1965–2013. Controls in the bottom panel are the 1960 real GDP per person and the 2013 unemployment rate. Sources: Penn World Tables Version 8.0 (Feenstra, Inklaar, and Timmer, 2015); World Bank 2015; Tanzi 2011; Organization for Economic Cooperation and Development 2015a, 2015e.

taxes or government spending on long-run economic growth, for similar reasons to those I point out above and below.[37] A few recent reviews argue that a consensus is emerging from the econometric literature that high overall levels of taxation do have negative effects on economic growth in the long run.[38] The fact that the authors of these reviews disagree suggests, at the very least, that claims of consensus are premature.

The lack of consensus should not be surprising given how many challenges are involved in efforts to produce convincing evidence on this question. We have already considered several reasons why it is difficult to tease out the long-run causal effect of taxes on economic growth from the data, but the problems don't end there.

One class of problems arises because there are many other confounding factors that could influence the level and growth of real GDP per person. To the extent that we can measure those other factors, we can control for them in a regression and solve the problem. But there are many factors that we would expect to affect economic growth that we can't measure, and if these factors are also changing over time in different countries in a way that is correlated with changes in taxes and the size of government, then our estimates will be biased.

Another, less commonly appreciated, problem is that adding control variables to a regression can give us a more inaccurate answer to the question we are interested in when those variables are channels through which the main explanatory variable of interest (in our case, taxation or government spending) influence the outcome (in our case, economic growth). For example, one way taxes might harm the economy is by reducing the incentive to save, invest, and accumulate capital and to supply labor. If we control for capital and labor supply in our regression, as economists who estimate growth regressions often do, then we might underestimate the negative effect of taxes on the economy. On the other hand, controlling for educational attainment or national saving might cause us to overstate the costs of high taxes, because facilitating public investment in education and promoting national saving (through the reduction of budget deficits) are channels through which high taxes might benefit the economy.[39]

Yet another critical class of problems arise because correlations in the data between economic growth on the one hand and tax revenues and government expenditure on the other might be driven by the business cycle and political responses to it, and this correlation might tell us nothing at all about the long-run economic effects of taxes and government spending. Referring back to the graph for the United States in figure 3.2b, we can see that log real GDP per person experienced lots of short-term fluctuations, most notably during the Great Depression in the 1930s, but more or less always returned to its long-run trend eventually.

The short-run fluctuations apparent in figures 3.2a and 3.2b are mainly temporary recessions and booms, which are primarily driven by fluctuating aggregate demand. For example, a drop in consumer confidence might cause consumption spending in the economy to fall, and the resulting increase in saving might not translate into demand for investment if the central bank fails to move the interest rate down enough to make that happen. The result is a recession, where reduced aggregate demand leads to unemployment and underutilized capital. But long-run economic growth is driven not by aggregate demand but rather by aggregate supply, which increases when we accumulate more and better capital, workers, and skills and when we achieve technological progress that enables us to use those resources more productively.

If our goal is to figure out whether permanently switching to a larger Nordic-style government would have costs in terms of lower GDP per person in the long run, we need our estimates to isolate how the incentive effects of taxes affect the long-run growth of aggregate supply, and we need to purge them of correlations that are about the temporary fluctuations of the business cycle. But that is hard to do econometrically, and depending on the technique used, econometric estimates might very well be dominated by those short-run effects.

The business cycle creates more concerns about reverse causality as well. When the economy falls into a recession, tax revenues automatically fall (for example, because people lose their jobs or their incomes shrink, pushing them into lower tax brackets) and government expenditures automatically rise (for example, because of increased spending on unemployment insurance benefits). This induces reverse causality from growth to taxes and government spending, which might obscure the causal effect of taxes and government spending on growth.

Some researchers have attempted to address this by focusing on the effects of tax revenues on economic growth, based on the supposition that the reverse causality described above would bias us against finding a negative effect of taxes on growth. If tax revenues automatically decline in bad economic times and go up in good times, this might be expected to induce a positive correlation between taxes and growth. In that case, we would have a conservative test of the causal effect of taxes, and if we nonetheless found a negative effect of taxes on growth, we could be more confident that any negative effect that we estimate is causal.

Unfortunately, things are considerably more complicated than that. Tax revenues tend to be lowest relative to GDP at the bottom of a recession (for example, because people have reduced incomes, which then fall into lower tax brackets). Politicians tend to amplify this by enacting tax cuts at the bottoms of recessions or when recovery is already underway, since there is a lag between when a recession is identified and when political action is taken. Recoveries from recessions tend to be periods of the highest economic growth, since it is easier to grow fast when the economy has significant unused capacity and can grow just by putting existing idle workers and capital to work. Growth in normal times, by contrast, requires the harder task of accumulating more capital, labor, and skills and improving technology.

When tax revenues are unusually low at the bottom of a recession, the econometrics used in many recent studies will tend to give the low taxes credit for the rapid growth that ensues in the recovery from the recession. This rapid growth might happen because tax cuts boost consumption spending and thus aggregate demand, helping to get a country out of a recession more quickly. However, even if a tax cut helps to get a country out of a recession and back to the economy's long-run trend sooner, that does not necessarily tell us anything about how taxes affect the long-run trend itself.

To illustrate why econometric evidence suggesting that taxes hurt long-run economic growth is not so convincing, let's consider two recent studies that are among the most up-to-date and best-done examples of studies reaching that conclusion. In each case, there are good reasons for skepticism about whether a long-run causal effect has really been identified.

In their study, Andreas Bergh and Martin Karlsson used panel data on twenty-nine currently high-income countries, most of them OECD nations but also including several countries that transitioned from developing to high-income status relatively recently, such as Singapore and Taiwan.[40] Each country was observed for a varying number of years, with the longest span being from 1970 through 2005. In an effort to purge short-run business cycle effects from the estimates, Bergh and Karlsson collapsed the data into a series of non-overlapping five-year averages and controlled for the unemployment rate. They also tried controlling for an array of other variables, including income per person at the beginning of each five-year period, average years of educational attainment, the national saving rate, the inflation rate, and an index of "economic freedom" (discussed below), among others.

The gist of Bergh and Karlsson's evidence, roughly speaking, is as follows. Holding certain other factors constant, when some countries increase their taxes as a percentage of GDP from one five-year period to another, their economic growth rate goes down by more across those time periods when compared to countries that did not change their taxes as a percentage of GDP over those same periods.[41] They estimated that an increase in taxes of 10 percent of GDP is associated with a reduction in the average annual growth rate of GDP of 1 percentage point.

While the Bergh and Karlsson study is a valiant effort, it still raises many questions. Some of the control variables in their analysis, such as educational attainment, are channels through which high taxes and big government might promote economic growth, so it is important to recognize that their estimate is, at best, an estimate of the economic cost of taxes after removing some of the economic benefit of what the taxes pay for. Still, their estimates would seem to imply that an increase in taxes that are used to pay for social transfers (which they do not include as a control variable) would have a negative effect on growth.

A big question about their study is whether that estimated effect of taxes on the growth rate is a temporary effect or a permanent effect. It matters a great deal whether increasing taxes by 10 percent of GDP reduces the growth rate of GDP by 1 percent a year for five years or by one percent per year forever, but we have no way of knowing which it is from their study. While collapsing the data into five-year averages and controlling for the unemployment rate might help reduce concerns that they are just estimating a short-run relationship between taxes and growth over the business cycle, it does not necessarily solve the problem. It could still be the case that their study is simply picking up on a tendency for tax revenues to be lowest at the troughs of recessions, which are then followed by rapid recoveries, in which case their estimates would really be about a correlation between low taxes and reversion of the economy to its long-run trend, and they wouldn't tell us anything about how taxes affect the long-term trend.

Moreover, the estimated effects of their study are highly inconsistent with what we find when we make comparisons over much longer spans of time. As figures 3.2 through 3.5 above attest, many rich countries increased taxes relative to GDP by a great deal over the last five or ten decades. As Peter Lindert has shown, the increased government revenue from these taxes was mostly used to expand social insurance. Yet there is no apparent correlation with lower growth rates over the long run.[42] The discrepancy between that and the effect estimated by Bergh and Karlsson might have arisen because Bergh and Karlsson's study just picked up a short-run business-cycle-related effect. The inclusion of countries like Singapore and Taiwan also raises concerns about sample selection bias of the sort discussed earlier.

In another study, Norman Gemmell, Richard Kneller, and Ismael Sanz analyzed panel data on seventeen OECD countries

from the early 1970s through 2004.[43] Gemmell and his colleagues estimated how changes in overall taxes as percentage of GDP correlate with changes in economic growth, while controlling for "productive" government spending (such as spending on education and infrastructure) and for the less distortionary forms of taxes (such as consumption taxes), among other things. They concluded that an increase in "distortionary" taxes (such as income taxes) relative to GDP, used to finance "unproductive" government expenditure (such as social insurance), will have a negative effect on the economic growth rate that will persist for a number of years. They admitted that it is difficult to determine exactly how long the effect persists given their data.

The econometric strategy that Gemmell, Kneller, and Sanz apply to distinguish long-run from short-run effects of taxes on growth is too technical to explain in detail here.[44] But the reasons for concern about the validity of their approach are easy to understand given the evidence discussed earlier in this chapter. A critical concern is that, as Gemmell and his colleagues demonstrate statistically, they analyzed a period of time and a sample of countries where both taxes as a percentage of GDP and economic growth rates were stationary. Changes in economic growth rates and in taxes relative to GDP during this period tended to be small and to reverse themselves over time, so there were no permanent changes in either variable. As a result, their study amounts to extrapolating from relationships between short-run changes in taxes and growth rates that keep reversing themselves in order to infer what the long-run effect of a tax change on growth would have been if the tax change had not later been reversed.

There are big questions about whether such extrapolations are valid. As figures 3.2a, 3.2b, 3.4a, and 3.4b demonstrate, most of

the large, permanent changes in the size of government relative to GDP in high-income countries were already complete by the early 1970s. The major changes had occurred in the 1960s and earlier. By focusing only on years after the large permanent changes in the size of government had already occurred, Gemmell, Kneller, and Sanz did not take advantage of the best available opportunity to determine whether permanent changes in taxes relative to GDP actually have long-run effects on GDP.[45]

One piece of evidence that corroborates these concerns is a study by Georgios Karras that examined panel data on eleven OECD countries from 1960 through 1992. Karras verified statistically that, during this period, taxes as a percentage of GDP were non-stationary, while the growth rate in real GDP per capita was stationary. This suggests that permanent increases in tax rates relative to GDP (which *were* enacted during the 1960s) could not be having a *permanent* negative effect on the growth rate. Karras estimated that a permanent increase in taxes as a percentage of GDP would have only a very temporary and modest negative effect on the growth rate, reducing the *level* of GDP per person permanently but only by a small amount.[46]

Where Is the Common Ground?

While some of the disagreement about whether high taxes have identifiable negative long-run economic effects reflects disagreement about the issues I've highlighted above, in some ways, the disagreements are not as large as they might at first appear. Peter Lindert, in his 2004 book, *Growing Public*, and in chapter 2 here, presents copious evidence that a large social welfare state is a "free lunch" in the sense that there is no detectable long-run

cost to it in foregone GDP. He argues that this makes sense partially because the countries with the biggest welfare states, especially the Nordic states, have adopted very efficient public policies in other regards. These include keeping tax rates on capital income relatively uniform and low, adopting broad tax bases with few deductions, relying heavily on relatively efficient value-added taxes, making large investments in education, subsidizing complements to work such as child care, and maintaining openness to free trade, among many other things.[47] The theory is that this has helped offset any negative incentive effects of high taxes.

Gemmell, Kneller, and Sanz and Bergh and Karlsson seem to agree with this general point. Gemmell and his colleagues find that "productive" government expenditures such as public investment in infrastructure and education have positive effects on economic growth that roughly offset the negative effects of taxes. They conclude:

> Hence, Jones's (1995) view that it would be an "astonishing coincidence" if two non-stationary variables that drive growth compensate for each other in such a way as to generate a stationary growth process, is not so astonishing in this context. Rather, our results largely confirm Dalgaard and Kreiner's (2003; p. 83) *a priori* conjecture that: "it may well be the case that a higher tax rate has a significant negative effect on the growth rate, but that this is roughly offset by a significant positive growth effect of the productive government expenditure that is financed by the higher tax rate, thus resulting in a small overall net effect."[48]

Relatedly, a major theme in Bergh and Karlsson is that uncovering the negative causal effect of taxes on economic growth requires controlling in a thorough way for all the other efficient policies and institutions that the large social welfare states, especially the Nordic countries, have adopted to help offset the hypothesized negative effects of high taxes. For instance, Bergh and Karlsson show that the estimated effect of taxes on economic growth in their 1970–2005 panel switches from a small positive to a large negative when they add the Fraser Institute's Economic Freedom Index (excluding the part that depends directly on government size)—which is basically a summary measure of the efficiency of government policy and its implementation—as a control variable.[49]

So, despite all the other reasons for disagreement noted earlier, if the question is posed as "Would the economy of a country like the United States suffer in the long run if it were to adopt the Nordic package of public policies wholesale?" we might actually have a consensus among these researchers that the answer is no. The researchers discussed here who find negative effects of taxes on growth are essentially arguing that the Nordic countries could have even higher economic growth if they maintained all their market-friendly policies but scaled back on their taxes and social welfare policies. That is plausible, but it has by no means been convincingly demonstrated.

It is also possible that the market-friendly policies adopted by the Nordic countries are only politically palatable and social welfare enhancing if implemented in conjunction with generous social programs and the high taxes that finance them. For example, economically efficient policies such as openness to free trade have the potential to expose people to considerable risk and to exacerbate the inequality of market incomes. So the high-tax, high–social insurance combination might be necessary to ensure that those efficient policies produce broadly shared prosperity and earn the support of voters.

EFFECTS OF TAXES ON LABOR SUPPLY

How do peoples' decisions about whether and how much to work respond to taxes? This is potentially one of the most important channels for taxes to harm economic efficiency. It is also one that cannot be avoided if we are to tie taxes to any feasible indicator of the ability to pay taxes. What does the evidence suggest?

Aggregate Cross-Country Evidence on
Taxes and Labor Supply

Let's start with evidence from comparisons across countries. These have the advantage of being relatively transparent. Moreover, Raj Chetty argues that such comparisons may be our best hope of estimating the true long-run effects of taxation on labor supply.[11] Chetty's point is that there are many frictions that stand in the way of optimally adjusting one's behavior to a change in incentives caused by the tax system, so such responses will only evolve slowly and in response to large changes in incentives. In that case, to detect the true long-run effect, we would need to compare situations where the incentives were very different over long periods of time.

What are the frictions? One is that people are rationally inattentive to taxes, since it is costly to pay attention to them and understand them. As a result, it is only worthwhile to learn about taxes' effects on incentives and respond to them when the change in incentives is big. Another is that many workers may have limited flexibility to unilaterally adjust their own labor supply, so that adjusting labor supply in response to changes in incentives caused by the tax code may require coordination and society-wide changes. Workers' ability to optimize their own labor supply may be limited by employers setting the terms of employment inflexibly, as in a mandated forty-hour workweek. This might be motivated by complementarities across workers, where each worker is more productive when he or she can count on being at work at the same time as his or her coworkers. Or it might be motivated by imperfect information, where employers cannot accurately assess an individual worker's productivity. In that case, an employer might consider an individual worker's expressed desire to work fewer hours than the social norm to be a signal that the worker is a slacker.[51]

Regardless of the source of such optimization frictions, if they exist and are important, then cross-country comparisons between countries with very different tax policies over long periods of time might enable us to detect effects of taxation on labor supply that would otherwise be obscured.

Edward Prescott has argued that a comparison of taxes and labor supply across countries implies that taxation involves very large costs in terms of economic efficiency.[52] His work is frequently cited by those who make the case for that conclusion in the popular press and in books written for general audience.[53] Prescott's analysis was based on a comparison of data from the 1970s and the 1990s on taxes and hours worked in the United States and a small number of other rich countries. Using those data, he pointed out that countries with higher taxes had lower average hours worked in the 1990s but that in the 1970s, when the differences in taxes were smaller, the number of hours worked were more similar. This suggests that the pattern in the 1990s was probably not explained by persistent cultural differences in the taste for leisure, since if that were the explanation, the same countries should have had lower hours worked in the 1970s too.

While Prescott's point about the cross-country evidence had some merit, the conclusion that the efficiency costs of taxes are very large was primarily driven by a theoretical model that involved arbitrary assumptions about the form of the utility function.[54] A subsequent study by Alberto Alesina, Edward Glaeser, and Bruce Sacerdote confirmed that average annual hours worked had tended to decline more between the 1960s and the mid-1990s in European nations than in the United States but argued that this might be explained by various confounding factors.[55] Principal among these was the fact that unions in many continental European countries pushed for mandatory reductions in work hours through extensive mandated vacation and paid leave, along with limitations on maximum hours worked per week. These union efforts tended to start in the 1970s and met with increasing success over time in terms of getting legislation enacted. The apparent motivation behind the unions' change in strategy was not a change in taxes but rather a misguided belief that reducing average hours worked per worker would open up more jobs.

It also must be emphasized that other public policies in European nations besides taxes reduce the incentive to supply labor. For example, many of these countries offer incentives for early retirement in their social security programs. Empirically, incentives for early retirement are indeed strongly correlated with earlier retirement across countries.[56] But there is no necessary reason for public pension schemes to be designed this way, so this is not a necessary cost of a generous welfare state.

In figures 3.6a and 3.6b, I revisit the question of how taxes are correlated with labor supply across countries, using scatterplots of data from a longer time span and for a larger number of countries than most previous studies.[57] In both figures, the measure of labor supply is total hours worked in the economy divided by the population aged fifteen to sixty-four, which will be affected by both the average hours worked per worker and the share of people who are working. The measure of taxes is total general government tax revenue as a percentage of GDP.

Figure 3.6a confirms a general pattern where countries with higher taxes as a percentage of GDP work less, but the relationship is hardly compelling evidence of a strong response. The regression line suggests that each 10 percent of GDP increase in taxes is associated with sixty-three fewer hours worked per year per working-age adult. At US levels of taxation and hours worked, that would imply that a 10 percent increase in after-tax wage would be associated with about a 4 percent increase in hours worked.[58] But the estimate is not statistically different from zero and has a wide confidence interval around it.

Figure 3.6b shows the percentage change in annual hours worked per person aged fifteen to sixty-four between the 1960s and the 2004–2013 period (I average over multiple years to help smooth out fluctuations due to the business cycle) plotted against the change in taxes as a percentage of GDP over the same period. Here, in contrast to some earlier research, there is no evident relationship across countries between the change in taxes and the change in labor supply over time. The slope of the regression line implies that an increase in taxes of 10 percent of GDP is associated with a 0.03 percent *increase* in hours worked, on average, with a 95 percent confidence interval ranging from negative 14 percent to positive 14 percent.[59]

To be sure, almost all of the countries with larger increases in taxes over time than the United States saw average hours worked drop significantly, whereas the United States saw almost no change since the 1960s in average hours worked per working-age

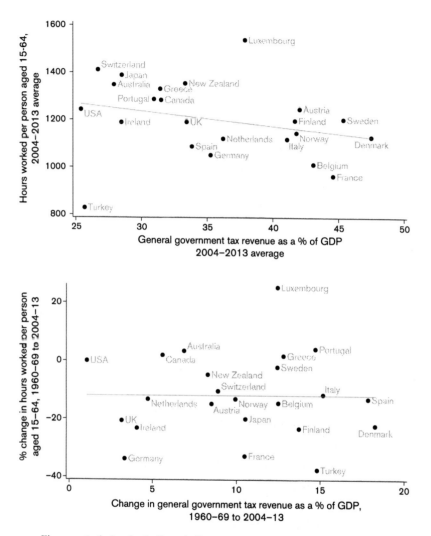

Figures 3.6a *(top)* and 3.6b *(bottom)*. Cross-country comparisons of hours worked and taxes as a percentage of GDP. In the bottom panel, data for Greece, Luxembourg, and Turkey for the earlier period are for 1965–1974. Sources: Conference Board 2015; World Bank 2015; Tanzi 2010; Organization for Economic Cooperation and Development 2015a, 2015e.

adult. But among the countries with big tax increases since the 1960s, there is no clear relationship between the size of the tax increase and the size of the decline in hours worked.

The location of many of the countries in the scatterplot in figure 3.6b seems consistent with Alesina, Glaeser, and Sacerdote's theories about the role of union strategies in influencing hours worked. For example, unions in Germany and France, but not in Sweden, pushed for "work sharing" and hours reductions of the sort that Alesina and his colleagues emphasized, and we can see that Germany and France experienced large percentage declines in hours worked since the 1960s, while Sweden experienced hardly any decline at all.[60]

In general, the comparison across countries at a fixed point in time in figure 3.6a is at least consistent with the hypothesis that taxes negatively influence hours worked, whereas the comparison of relative changes over time across countries in figure 3.6b is not. In neither case is there a relationship that is tight enough to merit statistical confidence. One reason the pattern relating higher taxes to less labor supply is much less stark here than Prescott's analysis implied is that Prescott used data on a much smaller set of countries for which the pattern happened to fit his hypothesis better.

Another reason why the correlation between taxes and labor supply is less pronounced in figures 3.6a and 3.6b than in some previous analyses is that, as Henrik Kleven has emphasized, cross-country data from the 1990s showed a much stronger negative relationship between taxes and the percentage of the adult population that was working than does more recent data.[61] Some of the weakening of the relationship in more recent data could be due to the confounding effects of the Great Recession, so this newer evidence should be interpreted cautiously. Nonetheless, Kleven uses data from 2009 and 2010 to perform a purely cross-sectional comparison across high-income countries, showing that, if we adjust our measure of tax rates to appropriately take into account the negative effects of means-tested transfers on incentives to participate in the labor force, there is now actually a strong *positive* correlation across countries between taxes and employment rates of people aged twenty to fifty-nine. In other words, in countries where taxes and means-tested transfers reduce the incentive to work by more, a *larger* share of the prime-age adult population is working, which certainly seems counterintuitive.[62]

Importantly, Kleven goes on to show that much of this puzzling pattern can be explained by the fact that countries where taxes and means-tested transfers tend to reduce the incentive to work the most also tend to do the most through government to offer subsidies that are complementary to labor supply, such as public support for child care, preschool, and elder care.[63] In Denmark, Sweden, and Norway, the value of such subsidies is in the vicinity of 6 percent of aggregate labor income.

Economic theory suggests that, if we can't tax leisure, then it can be economically efficient to subsidize complements to work as an indirect way of offsetting the inefficient incentive to take too much leisure and work too little. So this is yet another example where countries with high taxes and generous welfare states are implementing compensatory policies that help keep the costs in terms of economic efficiency low. While we could boost labor supply in a more efficient direction in either of two ways— by cutting taxes and means-tested transfers or by maintaining them while subsidizing child care and other complements to work—the latter approach would presumably be preferable in terms of social welfare, as it is likely to combine similar levels of efficiency with a greater degree of economic equality.

Econometric Evidence on Taxes and Labor Supply

Markus Jäntti, Jukka Pirttilä, and Håkan Selin performed the most careful econometric analysis to date that exploits the large relative changes over time in incentives to work across countries in order to understand how labor supply responds to incentives.[64] They used repeated cross sections of household- and individual-level data from the Luxembourg Income Study for thirteen OECD countries in various years between the 1970s and 2004. Jäntti and his colleagues estimated how changes in after-tax wages and non-labor income affect hours worked and labor force participation decisions in a way that relies entirely on relative changes over time in public policies, wages, and non-labor incomes across countries and across cells within countries defined by educational attainment, gender, and age.

The strategy used by Jäntti and his coauthors addresses many potential concerns about reverse causality, and many concerns about potential biases arising from unmeasurable influences on work effort that are correlated with after-tax wages. For instance, many prior studies of individual-level labor-supply decisions essentially estimate whether people who have higher wages because of higher educational attainment choose to work more hours as a result. A problem with that approach is that the choice to pursue more years of education is probably positively correlated with one's unobserved taste for work. If we see more educated people working more hours, it might be because they are responding to the incentive to work created by the higher wages they earn. Or it might occur because the types of people who tend to get more education also tend to be the types of people who have a stronger taste for hard work and market consumption as opposed to leisure.

In the strategy exploited by Jäntti and his colleagues, the evidence is based on comparisons like this: did people with a given level of educational attainment increase their hours of work more over time if after-tax wages for people in their educational group and country happened to increase more over time compared to people in educational groups and countries where after-tax wages did not increase so much over time? Presumably, the changes over time in after-tax wages for a given educational group in a given country are less likely to be correlated with the unobserved tastes for work of people in that group. Those tastes are likely to be fairly persistent for a given educational group in a given country over time, whereas the changes in wages and tax rates for the group are largely driven by changes over time in policy and market conditions that are plausibly unrelated to that education group's tastes

In a regression exploiting the quasi-experiment described above, Jäntti and his colleagues estimated that a 10 percent increase in the after-tax wage is associated with a 3 percent increase in hours worked.[65] A similar approach to estimating the effects of the financial gain from work (after taking into account wages, taxes, and transfers) relative to not working implies that a 10 percent increase in the gain from work is associated with a 1.2 percentage point increase in the probability of working for women and an 0.2 percentage point increase in the probability of working for men.

Taking into account both the hours worked response and the participation response, the evidence in the study by Jäntti, Pirttilä, and Selin suggests that a 10 percent increase in after-tax wage is associated with an increase in average hours worked per adult of 3 to 4 percent. This could still be biased upward by the story that Alesina, Glaeser, and Sacerdote tell, where changes in union strategies caused reductions in work hours, and the countries where unions followed those strategies happened to be among those with the largest increases in tax rates. Nonetheless, as studies on the effects of taxes on labor supply go, this is one of the more convincing ones.

The estimated responsiveness of labor supply to after-tax wages in the study by Jäntti and his colleagues is fairly consistent with what the most convincing previous empirical literature on this subject suggested.[66] In 2012, Raj Chetty and his coauthors wrote an influential review of quasi-experimental studies on the effects of taxes on labor supply, all of which exploited policy changes that altered incentives differently over time for different groups of reasonably comparable people. The reviewed studies suggested that, on average, a 10 percent increase in after-tax wage would be associated with about a 4 percent increase in aggregate hours worked, taking into account the effects on both participation decisions and decisions about how many hours to work.[67] Chetty went on to argue that, if we were to take optimization frictions into account, a reasonable estimate of the *long-run* effect of a 10 percent increase in after-tax wage on hours worked would be closer to a 5 or 6 percent increase in aggregate hours worked.[68] The claim that the effect would be larger in the long run was based partly on the evidence from aggregate cross-country comparisons, which seems less compelling now than it did at the time.

A study by Soren Blomquist and Laurent Simula helps us translate estimates of how labor supply responds to taxes into implications for deadweight loss.[69] According to that study, if a 10 percent increase in after-tax wage causes a 4 percent increase in hours worked, then the labor supply response to an across-the-board increase in taxes on labor income in the United States in 2006 would have caused $0.31 of deadweight loss per additional dollar of tax revenue raised. To put it another way, this suggests that about 24 percent of Arthur Okun's metaphorical bucket would leak out due to the labor supply response to a tax increase in the United States.[70]

If the responsiveness of labor supply to incentives was half as large, which is plausible if you believe that confounding factors such as the influence of unions are partly driving the cross-country relationships between taxes and hours worked, then the implied deadweight loss per dollar of revenue raised would be $0.13. That implies that only 12 percent of the bucket leaks out due to the labor supply responses to a tax increase. Thus, our best estimates of the responsiveness of work to incentives suggest that such responses do cause some deadweight loss but that the deadweight loss is fairly modest relative to the revenue raised, meaning that it might easily be outweighed by the benefits of whatever the revenue is used for.

It is important to emphasize that what limited credible evidence we have suggests that the responsiveness of labor supply to incentives is smaller than average for working-age males, especially those with high incomes and high education. This is important because high-education and high-income males account for a very large share of labor income and tax revenue.[71] Therefore, their behavior is particularly important for thinking about how leaky the bucket is.

A study by Robert Moffitt and Mark Wilhelm found that hours worked by high-income males in the United States did not respond to the large increase in their incentive to work that occurred when the Tax Reform Act of 1986 reduced the top income tax rate from 50 percent to 28 percent.[72] Another study by Costas Meghir and David Phillips found that labor force participation decisions of highly educated men in the United Kingdom exhibited little responsiveness to changes in the incentive to work caused by policy changes.[73] The broader literature corroborates the relatively low responsiveness of labor supply to incentives among prime-age males and suggests that empirical estimates of labor supply responsiveness tend to be higher than average for people with lower education, women, and those near retirement age. Many of the quasi-experimental studies emphasized in Chetty's influential literature reviews are based on the responsiveness of labor supply of lower-education women (for example, in response to changes in the Earned Income Tax Credit).

If the labor supply decisions of high-income men, who account for so much income and tax revenue, are indeed less responsive than average to incentives, then the percentage decline in aggregate labor income and tax revenue in response to a progressive tax increase could be considerably smaller than might otherwise be implied by the econometric estimates noted above, which are averages across people rather than across dollars of labor income. This, in turn, would imply correspondingly smaller deadweight loss per dollar of tax revenue raised.

If taxes do have at least some negative effect on labor supply, then why didn't the countries with the largest increases in taxes suffer any apparent loss of GDP as a result, as figures 3.1 through 3.5 above suggest? Part of the reason is that, as figure 3.6b shows, countries with bigger increases in taxes did not experience larger declines in hours worked on average. So, if the econometric studies are right that higher taxes have at least some negative effect on hours worked, something else must have changed that offset that effect. Government subsidies that are complements to work, such as those that finance childcare and elder care, could be part of the answer.

Some other factors that may have helped offset any economic costs from reduced labor supply are illustrated in figures 3.7a and 3.7b.[74] Figure 3.7a demonstrates that, since the early 1960s, productivity (GDP per hour worked) has on average increased more over time in high-income countries that had larger tax increases than in countries that did not. Peter Lindert has argued that this is partly because much of the decline in labor supply in the countries that increased taxes and transfers the most occurred among people who are likely to be low in productivity, such as very young people and low-education workers near retirement age.[75] Consistent with this, employment rates as of 2007 for men and women in the high-tax countries such as the United Kingdom and France were almost identical to those in the low-tax United States for people of the prime working ages of twenty-five to fifty-five, and they were only lower than in the United States for younger and older people.[76]

Another relevant consideration is that the average years of educational attainment went up significantly more over time in countries that had larger tax increases, which is demonstrated in figure 3.7b. People spending longer in school reduced labor supply temporarily by delaying entry in to the labor market, but at the same time it probably contributed to a faster rate of productivity growth because these people were building useful skills.

DO TAX CUTS FOR THE RICH CAUSE THEM TO EARN MORE PRE-TAX INCOME?

A reduction in hours worked caused by higher taxes is just one example of how the behavioral response to taxes can cause deadweight loss. More generally, the incentive effects of higher tax rates can lead to all sorts of other responses, such as employees

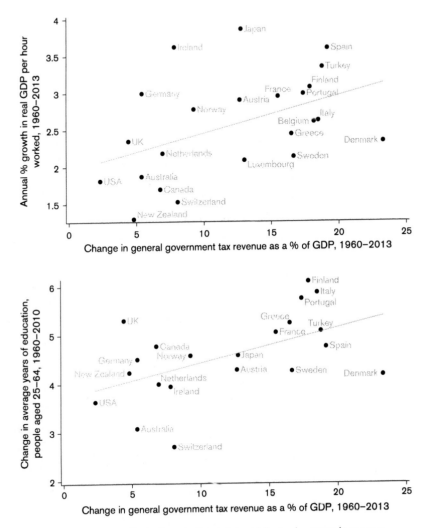

Figures 3.7a *(top)* and 3.7b *(bottom)*. Countries with larger increases in taxes as a percentage of GDP had larger increases in productivity and educational attainment, 1960–2013. Data for Greece, Luxembourg, and Turkey start in 1965. Sources: Conference Board 2015; Cohen, Leker, and Soto 2014; Tanzi 2011; Organization for Economic Cooperation and Development 2015a, 2015e.

being less productive during each hour worked, shifting to a different occupation that pays less or makes tax evasion easier, substituting toward forms of compensation or consumption that are more lightly taxed, engaging in less risk-taking or entrepreneurship, and hiring fancy lawyers to facilitate the use of tax shelters. Any of these responses can involve deadweight loss, and many of them will potentially show up in the data as observable changes in the amount of pre-tax income that one receives.

One strategy public finance economists use to uncover evidence of the efficiency costs of taxation has been estimating how changes in tax rates affect the amount of pre-tax income people earn and report to the tax authority. In particular, if some people get a big tax cut and others do not, does the reported pre-tax income of the people who got the tax cut go up relatively more? If so, that could be evidence of how incentives affect *all* of the margins of behavior mentioned above.[77]

This question is inextricably intertwined with the study of the causes of increasing inequality of pre-tax incomes, for reasons that figure 3.8 helps make apparent. The bottom panel shows that, between 1960 and 2014 in the United States, people in the top 0.1 percent of the distribution of pre-tax income benefitted from the largest cuts in marginal income tax rates compared to others in the top 10 percent. The top panel shows that people in the top 0.1 percent also experienced, *by far,* the fastest growth in pre-tax incomes, even when compared to the rest of the top 10 percent. If people in all parts of the income distribution had experienced similar income growth between 1960 and 2014, then all of the lines in the top panel would be flat lines at zero, as their shares of the nation's pre-tax income would not have changed. But this is far from being the case. The share of the nation's pre-tax income going to people in the top 0.1

percent of the income distribution grew by more than 250 percent between 1960 and 2014, whereas the share of pre-tax income going to those in the top 10 percent of the income the distribution outside the top 1 percent grew by only 26 percent.[78]

If we want to infer how tax cuts affect efforts to earn income, we might think of the people in the top 0.1 percent of the income distribution as a "treatment group" that was treated to a big cut in marginal tax rates over the period between 1960 and 2014. Similarly, we might think of people in the lower part of the top 10 percent of the income distribution as a "control group" that experienced a much smaller change in marginal tax rates, and this might tell us something about what would have happened to the pre-tax incomes of the top 0.1 percent if they too had experienced only a small change in tax rates. We then have something of a quasi-experiment.

If we believe this quasi-experiment is valid, it would suggest that cuts in marginal tax rates unleashed an explosion of productive income-earning effort at the top of the income distribution. That, in turn, would suggest that progressive income taxes cause a great deal of deadweight loss (i.e., it would be evidence of a very leaky bucket). On the other hand, there are lots of reasons to think this is *not* a valid quasi-experiment and that the patterns shown in figure 3.8 actually just reveal a coincidence, where non-tax factors that are driving rising inequality of pre-tax incomes happened to coincide in time with large tax cuts for top income earners.

Among econometric studies of the effect of tax cuts on income-earning efforts that exploit a quasi-experiment like the one shown in figure 3.8, the estimates are all over the map, depending partly on the strategies used to try to control for non-tax factors that could be driving rising pre-tax income

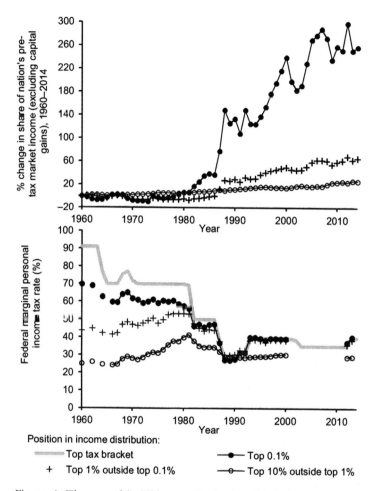

Figure 3.8. The parts of the US income distribution with the largest cuts in marginal tax rates also had the largest increases in pre-tax income, 1960–2014. Sources: Internal Revenue Service, Statistics of Income Division, 2014; Saez 2004; Urban-Brookings Tax Policy Center 2013a, 2013b; Piketty and Saez 2003 (tables and figures updated in 2015).

inequality. But some such studies do suggest a pretty large responsiveness of income-earning effort to incentives.[79] When economists want to argue that cutting tax rates on high-income people would have significant economic benefits, this is often the kind of evidence that they cite.[80]

A critical problem with such comparisons is that there are so many other plausible but hard-to-measure explanations for the patterns seen in figure 3.8. Unlike the tax incentive explanation, these alternative explanations do not imply that progressive taxes have large costs in terms of economic efficiency. Below, I review a few of the most plausible of these alternatives.[81]

One theory is that technology and globalization have been evolving in ways that complement the productivity of highly skilled people and enable them to serve wider markets around the world, increasing the demand for their services. For example, improved communications technology now enables the best entertainers, financiers, and business consultants to sell their services all around the world.

A second theory is that business executives, financial professionals, and others at the top of the income distribution have increasingly been engaging in "rent-seeking" behavior, meaning their efforts are directed toward the negative-sum game of redistributing wealth toward themselves instead of directing all their efforts to productive activities that create new wealth. For example, corporate executives may be exerting more effort to bargain and/or collude with their peers on the board of directors in order to redistribute income toward themselves and away from shareholders. This could take the form of executives persuading the board to grant them executive stock options in excess of what is necessary to induce the executives to exert optimal effort in the task of running the company. When we cut marginal income tax rates, that increases the incentive to engage in all sorts of efforts that lead to the receipt of more pre-tax income, whether they are economically productive or not.

A third theory points out that some of the increase in measured top incomes, which are based on data reported on personal tax returns, might simply be income that used to appear only on corporate tax returns in the past. Prior to 1986, top personal income tax rates were high relative to the corporate tax rate, so there was an incentive to shelter income in those corporations. Now that top personal rates have dropped sharply relative to corporate tax rates, there is more incentive to receive income through business forms that are only taxed on the personal tax return so as to avoid the corporate tax.[82] In that case, some of the rise in reported top incomes on personal tax returns is not a real increase in income at all; instead, income that was being created all along didn't formerly show up in the personal income tax return data, and now it does.

For these reasons, even people who are near the top of the income distribution are not a credible control group for evaluating the causal effects of tax cuts on the income-earning efforts of people at the very top of the income distribution in the same country. There are too many important factors, besides incentives to engage in productive economic activity, that might have been causing pre-tax incomes at the top and pre-tax incomes *near* the top to diverge over time. Any conclusion about the causal effect of taxes on productive income-earning efforts derived from a comparison like that in figure 3.8 should thus be viewed skeptically.

An alternative approach is to use people at the top of the income distribution in other countries, where tax rates were not cut so much, as a control group. The hope is that other non-tax factors that are driving greater pre-tax income inequality would be operating similarly across countries, which would enable us to tease out the independent effect of taxes. A 2014 article by Tomas Piketty, Emmanuel Saez, and Stefanie Stantcheva took this approach.[83] Figures 3.9a and 3.9b reproduce and update their basic analysis. Figure 3.9a shows that among the eighteen high-income countries for which comparable data are available over long periods of time, the countries that had larger cuts in top income rates since the 1960s also tended to experience larger increases in the share of the nation's pre-tax market income that goes to the top 1 percent.

The very tight relationship between changes in top marginal income tax rates and changes in top pre-tax income shares across countries in figure 3.9a implies that a 10 percent increase in the incentive to earn income (measured by 1 minus the marginal tax rate) is associated with about a 5 percent increase in the pre-tax incomes of high-income taxpayers.[84] If that were entirely due to an effect of incentives on productive economic activity, it would suggest that the revenue-maximizing top marginal tax rate in the United States would be about 58 percent (any increases beyond that would start to reduce revenue) and that the deadweight loss per additional dollar raised from a tax increase on a top bracket taxpayer in the United States in 2005 would have been $1.59.[85] That, in turn, would imply that when we impose taxes on top bracket taxpayers to transfer funds to benefit the less well-off, about 61 percent of the redistributive bucket leaks out due to deadweight loss.[86]

Piketty and his colleagues acknowledged that the strong relationship between changes in top marginal tax rates and changes in top income shares suggests that rising top pre-tax income shares probably have *something* to do with taxes. But they also

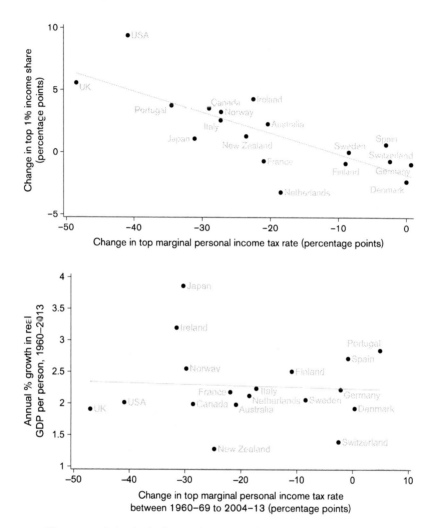

Figures 3.9a *(top)* and 3.9b *(bottom)*. Countries with larger cuts in top personal income tax rates had larger increases in top 1 percent pre-tax income shares, but similar growth in real GDP per person, 1960–2013. The top panel depicts the change in the ten-year average value of each variable from the earliest ten-year period for which data is available to the latest ten-year period for which data is available for each country between 1960 and 2013. Sources: Piketty, Saez, and Stantcheva 2014; Alvaredo et al. 2015; Organization for Economic Cooperation and Development 2015b; Penn World Tables Version 8.0 (Feenstra, Inklaar, and Timmer, 2015); World Bank 2015.

showed, in an analysis that I replicate here using slightly different and more up-to-date data in figure 3.9b, that there is *no* significant correlation across the eighteen countries between changes in top personal income tax rates and economic growth rates since 1960.[87] If a rise in top income shares caused by reduced top tax rates had corresponded to a rise in real productive economic activity by top income earners, we should be able to detect some positive effect of that on overall GDP per person. Yet neither figure 3.9b nor the battery of econometric estimates in their paper reveals any significant relationship.

To explain this disconnect, Piketty, Saez, and Stantcheva argued that some of the rise in top income shares must represent a rise in rent-seeking activity. The incentive to engage in such activity rises when tax rates are cut, but the rent-seeking activity fails to produce additional GDP and instead only redistributes GDP toward the rent-seekers. Piketty and his colleagues argued that corporate executives bargaining for higher pay without actually becoming more productive is an important part of the story.[88]

The plausibility of this phenomenon is bolstered by research I conducted with Adam Cole and Brad Heim. We found, through an analysis of IRS data on the self-reported occupations of taxpayers, that about 70 percent of the rise in the top 0.1 percent's income share between 1979 and 2005 in the United States can be explained by increased income going to people who call themselves executives, managers, or supervisors or who work in finance.[89] Moreover, among those in the top 0.1 percent, financial professionals had significantly faster income growth than almost any other occupation. Many of those people are in jobs that involve opportunities for behavior that might plausibly be characterized as rent-seeking.

Given available data, it is difficult to pin down precisely how much of rising top incomes reflects increases in productive economic activity as opposed to rent-seeking activity. Clearly, some of each is going on. There are many plausible stories and corroborating pieces of evidence suggesting that there is at least *some* rent-seeking at the top of the income distribution, but research on this question is still quite young. For example, in our paper, we showed that about 43 percent of people in the top 0.1 percent of the income distribution in 2005 called themselves executives, managers, or supervisors. But it is also clear that only some of these people work for publicly traded companies, while many others work for closely held businesses. So far, it is unclear exactly how many are in each group, and it is also unclear how much opportunity for rent-seeking (in the form of executives and managers of companies exploiting other owners) there is in each group. Presumably, the opportunities for rent-seeking are larger in publicly traded firms due to a larger free-rider problem in monitoring executive compensation, but firms that are not publicly traded can still have enormous numbers of owners, especially when they are organized in the form of a partnership.[90]

Another approximately 18 percent of people in the top 0.1 percent of the income distribution in 2005 were in finance. A number of authors have identified plausible reasons why the tremendous rise in finance as a share of GDP in recent decades may in part reflect redistribution away from financially unsophisticated individuals and toward financial professionals rather than toward value-creating activity.[91] For example, mutual fund managers earn high fees despite the fact that the fraction of fund managers that do better than the average return for the stock market as a whole, after adjusting for risk, is far less than would be predicted based on pure random chance. Part of the high pay of these fund managers may just reflect exploitation of customers' poor understanding of finance and psychological biases and irrationalities as opposed to socially productive effort.

Other professions well represented at the top of the income distribution could also be engaged in remunerative but unproductive activities to some extent. For example, doctors accounted for about 16 percent of the top 1 percent of the income distribution in 2005. Some portion of their incomes, on average, comes from exploiting their informational advantage to perform medical procedures that are of questionable value relative to their cost but are lucrative.[92] Lawyers account for another 8 percent of the top 1 percent, and some portion of their incomes reflect rent-seeking in the form of lobbying, collecting fees from patent-troll litigation, and so forth.[93] We can even expect spillover effects to other highly skilled occupations where rent-seeking is not possible, as those occupations will have to pay higher wages to compete with the rent-seeking occupations for talent. Obviously, there are lots of talented, skilled, and dedicated people in all of these professions who are contributing real value to society. But the idea that rent-seeking likely explains *some* portion of the skyrocketing incomes at the top of the distribution is hard to deny.

The lack of correlation between which countries had the fastest growth in incomes at the top of the income distribution and which countries had the fastest overall economic growth could be explained by other factors as well. For example, if cuts in top personal tax rates cause people to shift reported income from corporate to personal tax returns, it will show up as an increase in top income shares in the data but will produce no change in GDP. The important point for our purposes is that none of the alternative explanations—rent-seeking, technological change and globalization, or shifting of reported income between personal and corporate tax bases—implies that increasing tax rates on high-income people involves large costs in terms of economic efficiency.[94]

Based on the confidence intervals around the estimated relationship between change in top tax rates and economic growth across countries, Piketty, Saez, and Stantcheva infer that, at most, only 40 percent of the estimated relationship between top tax rates and income growth shown in figure 3.9a represents a response of productive economic activity to marginal tax rates. That implies that a 10 percent increase in the incentive to earn income of top income earners would be associated with only about a 2 percent increase in their real productive economic activity. If that were so, then the revenue-maximizing top tax rate in the United States would be 70 percent. Given the tax structure in place in the United States in 2005, the deadweight loss per additional dollar of tax revenue raised from a tax increase on top-bracket taxpayers would be $0.33.[95] That would imply that that about a quarter of an additional bucket of redistribution from top-bracket taxpayers would leak out.[96] If that were the case, then you might support raising tax rates on top-bracket taxpayers in order to finance something that makes people lower down in the income distribution better off, as long as you think a dollar is worth at least 1.33 times as much to the lower-income beneficiary as it is to the high-income taxpayer when considered in terms of happiness or ethical value.[97]

CONCLUSION

Government expenditure can have important benefits in terms of improving economic efficiency and social welfare, and the size of those benefits depends on the pervasiveness and importance of market failures, the degrees of economic inequality and inequality of opportunity, the roles of luck versus effort in determining incomes, and the effectiveness of government policy at addressing these issues. Costs include both the direct costs to taxpayers and the deadweight loss from behavioral responses to taxes.

Chapters 1 and 2 in this book provide arguments and evidence suggesting that the benefits of larger government in the United States would outweigh the costs if public policy is designed and implemented wisely. In this chapter, I dug a little deeper into what we can learn, mainly from cross-country comparisons over time, about the net effects of larger government and higher and more progressive taxes on measurable indicators of economic prosperity, labor supply, and efforts to earn income more broadly. The available pieces of evidence are far from perfect randomized experiments and so are subject to many competing explanations. But the most reasonable interpretation at this point is that the net economic costs of the growth in government in rich countries have so far been, at worst, quite modest.

CHAPTER FOUR

Thinking Sensibly about the Size of Government

LANE KENWORTHY

Although America's self-image and international reputation are as a nation of limited government—of laissez-faire—government has been intimately involved in the economy throughout the country's history.[1] Some government efforts have helped the economy grow. Others have helped ensure that economic growth benefits everyone, not just those with the most talent or luck. Americans up and down the socioeconomic ladder enjoy much higher living standards now than at the nation's founding, or even half a century ago, and government has played a major role in this achievement.

Since the 1930s, social programs have been a big part of government's expansion. As we get richer, we tend to want to spend more to insure against the risk of income loss or large expenses due to illness, accidents, job loss, family needs, old age, and more. We also tend to care more about fairness—we want everyone to have basic economic security and a minimally decent standard of living, and we want people from less advantaged circumstances to have a reasonable shot at reaching the middle class. It's therefore not surprising that over the past century we've created a host of public social programs, from Social Security in 1935 to the Affordable Care Act in 2010, and that government spending has increased significantly. In 1920, government expenditures amounted to 12 percent of the country's GDP. In the first decade and a half of this century, they've averaged 38 percent.[2]

Where should we go from here? That hinges on the answers to three questions. Is the country doing fine, or are we falling short of where we'd like to be? If we're falling short, can government help? If it can help, would doing so have adverse effects on other things we want, such as a healthy economy?[3]

Jon Bakija, Peter Lindert, Jeff Madrick, and I have tried to answer these questions in this book. Here, in brief, are our conclusions.[4]

FOUR SHORTFALLS

Over the past generation, America hasn't been doing nearly as well as it should and could in quite a few respects. Chapter 1 highlights four important ones.

First, we haven't invested sufficiently in the maintenance and improvement of the country's infrastructure. Our systems of transportation, energy, water, and communication are vital to a high quality of life and to economic vibrancy. We need to do more to preserve and upgrade them.

Second, too many Americans lack sufficient financial security, and in some respects this problem has been getting worse. The incomes of the least well-off are too low, and our progress in lifting them has slowed dramatically. A significant and rising share of households suffer large fluctuations or outright declines in income. Too many are vulnerable to large unexpected expenses.

Third, over the past generation, we've made no progress in improving opportunity for Americans who grow up in low-income households, and we may have even lost ground in this fight. Equal opportunity is one of our most cherished goals as a nation. More than 90 percent of Americans consistently agree, according to Pew Research Center polls, that "our society should do what is necessary to make sure that everyone has an equal opportunity to succeed."[5] Yet a child whose parents are on the bottom fifth of the income ladder has only a 30 percent chance of making it to the middle rung or higher, according to the most recent data. We can't expect to achieve fully equal opportunity, but we're surely capable of doing better than this.

Fourth, since the late 1990s, too little of the country's economic growth has reached the incomes of households in the middle and below. Wage levels for ordinary Americans have been virtually stagnant. Only employment growth—in the form of households adding a second earner—has made it possible for incomes to increase at all, and since the turn of the century, employment too has been at a standstill.

GOVERNMENT CAN HELP

Markets, families, and voluntary organizations are unlikely to get us very far in addressing these problems. Indeed, market developments are a key source of the pressures and strains on ordinary American households. As product market competition has intensified and computers and robots have proliferated, firms have faced greater pressure to reduce their workforce, hold wages in check, and pare back benefits. Meanwhile, families and voluntary associations have weakened. The share of American children who grow up with one parent or with a constantly changing cast of parents, partners, and stepparents has increased. Civil society organizations, from churches to parent-teacher associations to labor unions, have lost members and influence.

Government can't solve all of our problems, but as chapter 1 explains, it *can* help improve infrastructure, economic security, opportunity, and fairly shared prosperity. We know this from America's experience over the past century. Universal K–12 schooling, public universities and community colleges, the GI Bill, veterans benefits, Social Security, unemployment insurance, Medicare and Medicaid, disability benefits, the statutory minimum wage, the Earned Income Tax Credit, the Child Tax Credit, food stamps (SNAP), housing assistance, energy assistance, school lunches, training and job search programs, Head Start, and even the not-widely-beloved Temporary Assistance for Needy Families (formerly Aid to Families with Dependent Children), plus a host of others, are success stories. Some of these programs are huge; some are relatively small. Some work better than others. All of them require taxes, and all of them have some unintended adverse effects. But every one of these programs has improved living standards and fairness for ordinary Americans.

We also know from the experiences of other affluent nations that there are additional programs and program features that the United States could usefully adopt, such as fully universal health insurance, one-year paid parental leave, universal early education, a child allowance or more generous Child Tax Credit, very low-cost college education, paid sickness insurance, and more paid vacation days.

Expanding some of our existing social programs, adding new ones, and funding our infrastructure needs won't be cheap. As a rough estimate, and including increases in the cost of Social Security and Medicare that will come with the retirement of the baby boom generation, we're looking at adding perhaps 10 percent of GDP in government expenditures.

MORE GOVERNMENT SPENDING ON SOCIAL PROGRAMS AND INFRASTRUCTURE PROBABLY WON'T HURT THE ECONOMY

Logic tells us that there must be some point at which public provision of infrastructure and social programs will begin to harm the economy. If the taxation needed to fund this spending is too heavy, it will cause a reduction in investment and innovation. If the programs weaken employment incentives, fewer people will be in paid work. The result will be slower economic growth and thus a lower standard of living for everyone in the long run.

It would be nice if social scientists could locate the tipping point—the point beyond which public spending on social programs and/or infrastructure reduces economic growth—with a theoretical model or a computer simulation. Alas, we can't. We need empirical evidence.

There are many potential sources of such evidence: observational studies of individual behavior, experiments, comparisons across cities or regions, and more. The most informative, in our view, is examination of the experiences of countries over time. What we want to know is, if the United States increases public spending on infrastructure and social programs and raises taxes in order to pay for this spending, how much, if at all, will economic growth decrease? The most useful information for answering this question is what has happened when America and other rich, longstanding democratic nations have done this sort of thing in the past. This is a small and diverse set of countries, and they haven't been randomly assigned to groups in an experimental design, so we need to be cautious in drawing conclusions. But there is no substitute for trying to learn what we can from these countries' experiences.

Over the past 150 years, and particularly since around 1960, affluent democratic nations have made very different choices about the size of government. Beginning with little in the way of public social programs and with roughly similar levels of government expenditures and taxes, these countries experienced a large and persistent divergence in the size of their governments. If big government causes significant economic damage, we ought to be able to see that impact in these nations' economic growth patterns.

Chapter 2 examines what countries' experiences tell us about the effect of public social programs—the welfare state—on economic growth. Nations with more generous welfare states tend to have lower poverty rates, lower income inequality, less gender inequality, longer life expectancy, and greater happiness. They have achieved this without any apparent reduction in economic growth. A welfare state sized and structured like those in countries such as Sweden, Denmark, and Norway has so far turned out to be, in the lingo of economists, a "free lunch." It gives us a more fairly distributed economic pie without reducing the size of the pie.

Why has the large welfare state proved to be a free lunch? We don't know for certain. It may be because the types of taxes these countries use to pay for heavy government expenditures are cheap to administer and create little or no disincentive for work and investment. It could be that generous social protections encourage risk-taking, innovation, and the acceptance of globalization and new technology. Maybe these countries' heavy reliance on universal benefits improves societal cohesion. Perhaps their healthcare systems ensure a more productive labor force. Maybe egalitarian wages and incomes encourage more work effort and loyalty to employers. Perhaps their public social programs help to better develop and utilize women's human capital.

Some continental and southern European nations have had slower economic growth than the United States over the past generation. While opponents of a large welfare state point to this as evidence that those nations have passed the tipping point mentioned above, the economic struggles of those countries owe largely to excessive protection of vested interests against competition in product and labor markets, not to the welfare state.

Chapter 3 looks at whether the overall size of government, in terms of expenditures and taxes, has reduced economic growth. Data going back to 1870 are available for twelve major industrialized countries. In the century and a half since then, government expenditures as a share of GDP have risen sharply in these countries. Yet they didn't experience a slowdown in their long-run economic growth rates. The fact that economic growth has been so stable over this lengthy period, despite huge increases in the size of government, suggests that government size probably has had little or no impact on growth.

If we compare across these countries, the evidence suggests that the ones with bigger increases in government expenditures since the late 1800s experienced similar—possibly faster, at worst only marginally slower—rates of economic growth over this period compared to those with smaller increases in government size. A good bit of the divergence across rich countries in government spending and tax levels occurred after 1960, and in this more recent period we have data for more countries. Here too we observe that nations with larger and smaller increases in government size had similar economic growth rates.

Other social scientists have attempted to estimate the effects of the overall level of taxes and/or government spending on economic growth since 1960, often using sophisticated econometric techniques and attempting to control for other determinants of economic growth. A few of these researchers have concluded that larger government is associated with slower economic growth. But these findings might be wrong: there are reasons to worry about whether this type of analytical strategy gets us closer to the truth than a simpler approach, and each of these studies has questionable elements. Even if they are right, their finding is that high levels of government taxation or spending reduce economic growth but that the programs these taxes and expenditures pay for increase economic growth, with the net result that the economies of big-government countries have grown just as rapidly as those of not-so-big government countries. So if the question is "Would the long-run economic growth of a nation like the United States decrease if it were to adopt the Nordic package of public social programs and the taxes needed to fund them?" it appears there is a near-consensus among researchers that the answer is "Probably not."

To sum up: The evidence available for assessing the effect of public social programs and overall government taxes and expenditures on economic growth isn't perfect, so it's impossible to offer a definitive conclusion. But the most reasonable judgment at this point is that the economic harm from big government in rich democratic nations has been nil, or at worst very modest.

WHAT LIES AHEAD

Will America move toward bigger government? That depends on what citizens want, what they ask for, the partisan balance of power in government, the relative strength of organized interests outside the electoral arena, circumstance, luck, and a host of other factors. These are difficult to predict, and it isn't our goal here to try to do that.[6]

Our aim with this book has been to examine the best available evidence on the impact of government size on the economy. Our conclusion is that increased government spending on infrastructure and social programs would benefit many ordinary Americans, and it would cause very little, or more likely zero, economic harm.

NOTES

This book was inspired by a conference sponsored by the Bernard L. Schwartz Rediscovering Government Initiative.

1. CAN GOVERNMENT HELP?

1. See Kulikoff 1992.

2. See, in general, Bourgin 1989.

3. Lawrence Summers cast doubt on industrial policy's uses in an interview for Daniel Yergin's book *The Commanding Heights*, a paean to market economics.

4. See, in general, Sellers 1994.

5. See, for example, Burnstein 2006.

6. For a contentious history that blames the New Deal for the Great Depression, see Shlaes 2008.

7. Fishback et al. 2007.

8. Cooper 2012; American Society of Civil Engineers 2013; Federal Highway Administration 2014; Anderson and Perrin 2015; Kanter 2015; Federal Communications Commission 2015.

9. Soltas 2013.

10. World Economic Forum 2015.

11. Congressional Budget Office 2011; Zandi 2011; Leduc and Wilson 2012.

12. Cooper 2012.

13. This section and the next two sections draw from Kenworthy 2014, chs. 2 and 3.

14. Lebergott 1976; Cox and Alm 1999; DeLong 2009; Fischer 2010, ch. 2.

15. Moss 2002; Castles et al 2010.

16. Kenworthy 2016a. This figure is for posttransfer-posttax income. Data are from the Luxembourg Income Study 2015, series DHI, using data from the US Census Bureau's Current Population Survey. Household income is adjusted for household size (each household's income is divided by the square root of the number of persons in the household) and then rescaled to reflect a three-person household. See Luxembourg Income Study 2015.

17. Rector 2007; Eberstadt 2008.

18. Edin and Lein 1997; Ehrenreich 2001; DeParle 2004.

19. Edin and Shaefer 2015.

20. Kenworthy 2016a.

21. Congressional Budget Office 2008; Gosselin and Zimmerman 2008; Hacker and Jacobs 2008; Jensen and Shore 2008; Acs, Loprest, and Nichols 2009; Rose and Winship 2009; Dynan 2010; Dynan, Elmendorf, and Sichel 2012; Winship 2012; Institution for Social and Policy Studies 2013.

22. Elizabeth Jacobs, pers. comm. Jacobs used Panel Study of Income Dynamics (PSID) data for her calculation. Mark Rank, Thomas Hirschl, and Kirk Foster did a related calculation also using PSID data. They asked what share of Americans experience five or more total years of income below the poverty line, of welfare receipt, or of unemployment between the ages of twenty-five and sixty. The answer was 35 percent. See Rank, Hirschl, and Foster 2013.

23. Kenworthy 2016f.

24. Morduch and Schneider 2014; Pofeldt 2014.

25. Kenworthy 2016f.

26. Mendes 2012. Mendes used Gallup data in her calculations.

27. Kenworthy 2016a, 2016d, 2016f.

28. Kenworthy 2015.

29. Hays 2003; DeParle 2004, ch. 14; Morgen, Acker, and Weigt 2010.

30. DeParle 2012; Shaefer and Ybarra 2012.

31. Authors' calculations using OECD data.

32. Diamond and Orszag 2004; Ruffing 2011; Aaron 2013.

33. Wolff 2011, table 4.1.

34. Center for Retirement Security 2009. These calculations used data from the Survey of Consumer Finances.

35. *Economist* 2008; Ghilarducci 2008; Wolff 2011; Fletcher 2013.

36. Graetz and Mashaw 1999; Munnell 2012; US Senate Committee on Health, Education, Labor, and Pensions 2012.

37. Heymann et al. 2009.

38. Bureau of Labor Statistics 2015. These calculations used data from the Bureau of Labor Statistics' March 2015 National Compensation Survey.

39. Ferrarini and Duvander 2010.

40. US House Committee on Ways and Means 2014.

41. Anrig 2006.

42. Kletzer and Litan 2001; LaLonde 2007.

43. Klein 2007; Reid 2009; Davis, Schoen, and Stremikis 2010; Organization for Economic Cooperation and Development 2011.

44. Because the data requirements are stiff—we need a survey that collects information about citizens' incomes and other aspects of their life circumstances and does the same for their children, for their children's children, and so on—we have less information about relative intergenerational income mobility than we would like. The best assessment of this type, the Panel Study of Income Dynamics, has been around only since the late 1960s.

45. The following discussion draws on Wilson 1978, 1987, 1996, 2009; Jencks and Mayer 1990; Fischer et al. 1996; Duncan and Brooks-Gunn 1999; Mayer 1999; Lareau 2003; MacLeod 2009; Currie 2011; Duncan and Murnane 2011; Kenworthy 2016c.

46. Economic Mobility Project 2012. For more about inequality of opportunity in the United States, see Kenworthy 2016c.

47. Hauser et al. 2000.

48. Ellwood and Jencks 2004; Cherlin 2009; Murray 2012; Parlapiano 2012.

49. Duncan, Ziol-Guest, and Kalil 2010; Kaushal, Magnuson, and Waldfogel 2011; Cooper and Stewart 2013.

50. Kornrich and Furstenberg 2013, table 3. These calculations used data from the Consumer Expenditure Survey.

51. Mayer 1999; Lareau 2003; Phillips 2011; Cooper and Stewart 2013.

52. Lareau 2003; Putnam 2015, ch. 3.

53. Jacob and Ludwig 2008; Altonji and Mansfield 2011.

54. Jencks and Mayer 1990; Wilson 1987, 1996; Sampson 2012; Sharkey 2013; Putnam 2015.

55. Jencks 2009; Bailey and Dynarski 2011.

56. Western 2006.

57. Wilson 1987, 1996; Wright and Dwyer 2003; Autor 2010; Western and Rosenfeld 2011; Blinder 2009.

58. Schwartz and Mare 2005.

59. Esping-Andersen 2004, 2011; Ermisch, Jäntti, and Smeeding 2012; Esping-Andersen and Wagner 2012.

60. Heckman 2008; Esping-Andersen 2009, 135–136; Ruhm and Waldfogel 2011.

61. Gornick and Meyers 2003; Organization for Economic Cooperation and Development 2006; Esping-Andersen 2009.

62. Vandell and Wolfe 2000; Waldfogel 2006. Approximately 28 percent of three- and four-year-olds are enrolled in public prekindergarten, and 52 percent are enrolled in some type of prekindergarten school. See Barnett et al. 2011, table 4; National Center for Education Statistics 2012, table A-1-1.

63. See Bowen, Chingos, and McPherson 2009; Hout 2009; Jencks 2009; Arum and Roksa 2011; Dynarski and Scott-Clayton 2013; National Commission on Higher Education Attainment 2013.

64. Jencks 2009, A7.

65. Organization for Economic Cooperation and Development 2010, table B5.1; 2012.

66. Duncan, Ziol-Guest, and Kalil 2010.

67. Waldfogel 2009, 52.

68. Kenworthy 2016e.
69. Mishel and Shierholz 2013.
70. Kenworthy 2008.
71. Kenworthy 2011, ch. 7; 2016a.
72. Kenworthy 2016e.
73. Kenworthy 2008, 2016b; Kleven 2014.
74. Organization for Economic Cooperation and Development 2015d, Statistical Annex, table B.
75. Ben-Galim and Dal 2009.
76. Freeman and Gottschalk 1998.
77. Kenworthy 2011, ch. 7.
78. For more on this idea, see Kenworthy 2013. This is similar in spirit to Robert Shiller's proposal for "inequality insurance"; see Shiller 2003, ch. 11.
79. Another possibility would be to index the EITC to average compensation, which would to rise in line with GDP per capita. See Pessoa and Van Reenen 2012.
80. To be effective, the EITC needs to be coupled with a rising minimum wage. Without a wage floor, an earnings subsidy may lead to reductions in low-end wage levels, which will offset the improvement in income achieved by the subsidy. This can happen in two ways. First, if the subsidy succeeds in pulling more people into work, the increase in competition for jobs will put downward pressure on wages. Second, regardless of labor supply, employers will be tempted to incorporate the value of the subsidy into the wages they offer. For more on this, see Kenworthy 2011, ch. 5.
81. Kenworthy 2014, 73–81.
82. Baker 2011, ch. 10.
83. Roin 2009.
84. Baker 2011, ch. 10.
85. Baker 2011, ch. 10.
86. Weeden 2002; Carpenter et al. 2012.
87. Avent 2011; Glaeser 2011; Yglesias 2012.
88. Baker and Moss 2009; Stiglitz 2009; Baker 2011, ch. 9; Zingales 2012.

2. ARE GOVERNMENT SOCIAL PROGRAMS BAD
FOR ECONOMIC GROWTH?

1. Smith (1766) 1978, 530–531. I am indebted to Barry Weingast for bringing this passage to my attention.

2. Smith (1776) 1993, 130–134, 420–434, 443. Smith was certainly prescient about taxpayers financing of the bulk of primary education. All of the countries with leading educational programs followed the same formula of funding mass schooling primarily with local taxes. Thomas Jefferson agreed with Adam Smith about the need for taxes to support public schooling (Butts 1978, 26–28), as did Milton Friedman in his book *Capitalism and Freedom*.

3. Smith (1776) 1993, 413, 443.

4. This chapter defines "social transfers" as taxpayer-funded government expenditures on health care, pensions, family assistance (America's welfare), unemployment compensation, active labor-market spending (retraining, etc.), and public housing subsidies. My definition of social transfers nearly matches the official OECD definition of "public social expenditure." The main difference between the OECD's definition and my own is that I would, whenever the data permit, exclude the pension benefits paid to public employees. These are part of labor contracts, comparable to private labor contracts, and are not redistributions from the rest of society. The OECD's database allowed such a separation in its social expenditure series for 1960–1981, but its current series starting in 1980 does not.

I define "social expenditures" as these social transfers plus public spending on education. This broader definition matches the definition used by Garfinkel, Rainwater, and Smeeding (2010).

My arbitrary definition of a "welfare state" is any democratic country for which public social transfers, and the taxes implicitly paying for them, exceed 20 percent of GDP. Had I defined the welfare state as any country devoting more than 20 percent of GDP to social spending, including public education spending à la Garfinkel, Rainwater, and Smeeding 2010, it would have been easier to show (as they do) that the welfare state is not bad for economic growth. For rhetorical purposes, I prefer the more stringent test focusing on social *transfers*, which are more controversial and less obviously productive than public expenditures on education, which I separate from my discussion of the welfare state.

My focus is on *public* social transfers. In some countries, such as the United States, tax provisions encourage private social expenditures by employers, particularly on health insurance and pensions (Adema, Fron, and Ladaique 2014). I don't include these here because the hypothesized redistributive effects, market distortions, and efficiency reductions are likely to be different than for public expenditures and because data for private social expenditures are available only for the years since 1995.

5. See Lindert 2004, chs. 10 and 18, and the downloadable data sets available either from Cambridge University Press (see the book's preface) or from the author's home page: http://economics.ucdavis.edu/people/fzlinder/peter-linderts-webpage/peter-lindert.

6. For a review of rates of economic return on education around the world, see Psacharopoulos and Patrinos 2004a, 2004b, and the earlier studies cited by them.

7. This second bias shows up even in the set of econometric panel tests that seems the best candidate for an objective discovery of negative growth effects: the overlapping studies by Kneller, Bleaney, and Gemmell (1999) and by Gemmell, Kneller, and Sanz (2011). The authors did not put any weight on the negative result about social spending, but that negative implication from their study should be taken seriously. With their help, I have found that even their best-practice econometric test has trouble identifying the shocks that we know were there, given our reading of recent history. For example, we know that at the start of the 1990s, Finland suffered a major macro-shock from the collapse of its main trading partner (the Soviet Union) and from misguidedly pegging the Finnish markka to the soaring German mark. Yet these authors' tests have no way of picking up such idiosyncratic, large macro-shocks that are neither time-fixed effects for all countries nor fixed county effects for all times. The result is a misleading correlation between Finland's huge safety net expenditures and the plummeting of the country's GDP. I thank Richard Kneller for making the data of these studies available.

8. On the growth (non)effects of progressive fiscal redistribution, measured by changes in Gini coefficients, see Lustig 2011; Wang, Caminada, and Goudswaard 2012; and Ostry, Berg, and Tsangarides 2014. For the non-effects of overall government size, see Jon Bakija's evidence in ch. 3 of this book.

9. Here is a rough quantification of the points listed in this section. Data from twenty-three countries circa 2007 show that the share of social transfers in GDP, our welfare state indicator, has these correlations with social achievements: (a) -0.56 with the share of households having less than 40 percent of median household income; (b) +0.39 with life expectancy; (c) +0.21 with Transparency International's clean government indicator; and (d) no overall correlation (0.01) with government budget surplus in 2007–2009. Correlations (a) through (c) are statistically significant at the 5 percent level.

10. See Wang, Caminada, and Goudswaard 2012 for information about OECD countries' inequality in 2004. For a readable and balanced summary of the definition of equality in terms of "vertical equity" and the case for progressivity in redistribution, see Slemrod and Bakija 2016, especially ch. 3.

11. On poverty shares relative to median incomes, see Organization for Economic Cooperation and Development 2008, 127. International comparisons of absolute poverty are found in studies by the Luxembourg Income Study; see Smeeding, Rainwater, and Burtless 2000; and Scruggs and Allan 2005.

12. Transparency International's index of clean government, called the "Corruption Perceptions Index," can be found at www.infoplease .com/world/statistics /2007-transparency-international-corruption-perceptions.html.

13. For statistics on government budget surpluses as shares of GDP in 2007 and 2009, see IMF eLibrary: http://data.imf.org.

14. For information about international differences in expressions of happiness, see the World Values Survey, which can be found at www.nationmaster.com/graph/lif_hap_net-lifestyle-happiness-net.

15. For a general discussion of this point, see Lindert 2004, chs. 4, 10, and 12; and Pestieau 2006, 81–83.

16. See, for example, Reinhardt 2000; Woodlander, Campbell, and Himmelstein 2003; and Kotlikoff and Hagist 2005.

17. Lindert 2004, ch. 3; Lindert 2014.

18. This omits, of course, the resource cost to taxpayers themselves of preparing their tax returns.

19. See Kato 2003; and Lindert 2004, chapter 10.

20. The closest things to econometric support for this conventional hunch are the results of studies by Kneller, Bleaney, and Gemmell (1999) and Gemmell, Kneller, and Sanz (2011), which indicate that indirect taxes are better for growth than direct taxes.

21. Thomasson 2002, 2003.

22. Eggleston and Fuchs 2012.

23. See, for example, the international data in the OECD Family Database, which can be found at www.oecd.org/social/family/database .htm. For other summaries of differences in parental leave laws and public infant care, see Lindert 2004, vol. 1, 252–257, 282–287.

24. See Madrick 2011, especially 286–404.

25. Lindbeck and Snower 1988, 2001; Flanagan 1988, 1999; Allard and Lindert 2007.

26. Organization for Economic Cooperation and Development 2008, ch. 5, figure 5.5 (updated September 12, 2008).

27. See Lynch 2001, 2006.

28. Carneiro and Heckman 2003; also see the sources they cite.

29. The trend toward earlier male retirement has reversed itself in many OECD countries since 2000.

30. On the recent acceleration of senior survival rates, see Eggleston and Fuchs 2012.

31. This result is derived from a budget-balancing equation in Lindert 2004, vol. 1, 195–196.

32. I have oversimplified Sweden's system, which is well described in Knuse 2010. Instead of using an index tied to GDP per working-age adult, Sweden uses two other index factors that yield a similar result. The economic aggregate is wages and salaries per employed person, not GDP per person aged eighteen to sixty-four. And Sweden backs up its pension stability with an additional trigger that goes off

whenever the pension fund's "balance ratio" (i.e., capitalized assets divided by capitalized obligations) drops below 1.

3. WOULD A BIGGER GOVERNMENT HURT THE ECONOMY?

I would like to thank Melissa Caplen for outstanding research assistance and Peter Pedroni, Joel Slemrod, and Lant Pritchett for helping me think more clearly about some of the issues in my chapter.

1. A thoughtful person might respond to this example by saying, "Hey, isn't it possible that the tax would make you work *harder?*" It is true that any tax that is related to ability to pay has both an income effect (the tax makes you poorer, which induces you to work harder to make up for it) and a substitution effect (the tax reduces the incentive to work by making market consumption relatively more expensive compared to leisure). Whether a tax causes you to work more or less does indeed depend on which of these two countervailing effects is stronger. However, the deadweight loss of a tax is entirely about the substitution effect, and any tax that has a substitution effect involves deadweight loss, even if there is an offsetting income effect. To see why, consider the only kind of tax that causes no deadweight loss at all—a lump-sum tax, which is a tax of a fixed amount that does not change, no matter how you change your behavior. Such a tax would mean that the rich and poor alike would pay the same dollar amount of tax. If we were to replace a labor-income tax with a lump-sum tax that raised the same amount of revenue from you, there would still be an income effect that would encourage you to work more, but there would be no substitution effect that would encourage you to work less because the tax would no longer depend on how much you work. In that case, the harm to you from the tax would be exactly equal to the tax revenue collected by the government, and there would be no deadweight loss. Moreover, compared to a lump-sum tax that raises the same amount of revenue, the labor-income tax would encourage you to work less because the income effect is the same in both cases, but only the labor income tax would have a substitution effect. Deadweight loss is fundamentally the extra economic cost that comes from

operating a system where taxes increase with ability to pay relative to what would happen with lump-sum taxes that raise the same revenue. The further that taxes get from lump-sum taxes, i.e., the more that taxes mitigate economic inequality, the larger the deadweight loss is. For a more formal diagrammatic demonstration of this point, see, for example, Rosen and Gayer (2009, ch. 15).

2. For example, a progressive consumption tax could be designed to raise the same tax revenue as our current tax system and to do about as much as the current system does to mitigate economic inequality without distorting incentives to save or invest or distorting incentives regarding which types of investment to do. See Slemrod and Bakija (2016) for further discussion of options for fundamental tax reform and their pros and cons.

3. Okun 1975.

4. For further discussion of the relevant issues here, see Okun 1975, Saez and Stantcheva, 2016; Diamond and Saez 2011; Mankiw, Weinzierl, and Yagan 2009; Kaplow 2008; Arneson 2012; Roemer 1998; Dworkin 2000; Rawls 1971; and Layard, Mayraz, and Nickell 2008.

5. Heckman (2012) offers an accessible discussion of evidence that investments in high quality preschool for children from disadvantaged homes have a high long-run economic payoff. Furman (2015) discusses a variety of credible empirical studies presenting evidence of long-term economic payoffs from a variety of social programs that involve investment in children from disadvantaged backgrounds. Stiglitz and Weiss (1981) offer the seminal theory for why asymmetric information can cause credit markets to fail, which in turn causes people without sufficient collateral to undertake less than the economically efficient amount of investment. The Organization for Economic Cooperation and Development (2015b) reviews arguments and evidence for why policies that reduce economic inequality can have economic benefits.

6. A full discussion of market failures and their implications for government policy can be found in any undergraduate public finance textbook, including, for example, Gruber 2013; Stiglitz and Rosengard 2015; and Rosen and Gayer 2009.

7. The 59 percent figure is from Center on Budget and Policy Priorities (2015) and includes 24 percent for Social Security, 24 percent for

health insurance programs such as Medicare, Medicaid, CHIP, and Affordable Care Act exchange subsidies, and 11 percent for safety net programs such as unemployment insurance, food stamps, and the refundable portion of the earned income tax credit, among other programs.

8. See Frick (2015) for an argument along these lines. Kenworthy (2014, ch. 4) presents evidence that the pace of innovation in the United States was at least as strong during the 1950s and 1960s, when economic inequality was much lower than it is today, and that observable indicators of innovation in Nordic countries have been robust and comparable to those in the United States in recent times.

9. That GDP is an imperfect measure of well-being is not a novel insight to economists. GDP is not intended to measure social welfare. Essentially, every introductory macroeconomics textbook begins with a discussion of this. See, for example, Frank and Bernanke 2013.

10. The quote is from Slemrod (2006, 82–83). Here and throughout this chapter, I define "taxes" to include "social contributions," where the latter involve mandatory payments to the government that are related in some way to benefits received, as is the case of the social security payroll tax in the United States. Certain data sources sometimes separate out social contributions from taxes, but in those cases I combine the data on taxes and social contributions.

11. Gadanne and Singhal 2014.

12. For a scatterplot that just includes OECD countries, which also demonstrates a strong positive correlation between taxes as a percentage of GDP and GDP per person, see chapter 4 of Slemrod and Bakija's (2016) book.

13. Gordon and Li (2009) show that low-income countries and high-income countries have similar statutory tax rates on average, but the low-income countries collect much smaller fractions of GDP as tax revenue. The low revenue yield for a given tax rate in low-income countries reflects some combination of rampant tax evasion and a larger share of economic activity (such as income earned below tax-filing thresholds) being legally exempt from taxation, the latter of which is partly motivated by the administrative difficulty of enforcing taxes on that activity. Robinson and Slemrod (2012) and Kleven (2014) also show

that, among relatively high-income countries, there is a strong positive correlation between tax collections as a percentage of GDP and objective measures of a country's ability to effectively administer a tax system, such as the fraction of economic activity that is subject to third-party information reporting to the tax administration.

14. Wagner (1883) 1958.

15. Slemrod 1995.

16. "Panel data" in this context means that multiple countries are followed over time, as opposed to "cross-section" data, which compares across countries at a given point in time.

17. According to data from the Penn World Tables Version 8.0 (Feenstra, Inklaar, and Timmer 2015), extended from 2011 through 2013 with data from World Development Indicators (World Bank, 2015), the countries experiencing the fastest growth in real GDP per person on average between 1960 and 2013 were mainland China, Equatorial Guinea, Botswana, South Korea, Singapore, Thailand, and Hong Kong. Taiwan also had a comparably high growth rate but is not represented in the Penn World Tables.

18. This point is emphasized by Agell, Ohlsson, and Thoursie (2006) and applies in particular to such studies as those conducted by Folster and Henrekson (2001) and Bergh and Karlsson (2010).

19. Rodrik (2007) offers a detailed discussion of the various ways that recent success stories of the economic growth of developing countries have not always followed doctrinaire free-market scripts, and Hausmann, Pritchett, and Rodrik (2005) and Pritchett and Werker (2012) offer interesting analyses of what sorts of policy and institutional changes preceded sustained rapid episodes of growth in developing countries. There is no evidence that the sustained growth takeoffs were generally preceded by significant tax cuts.

20. In figures 3.2a and 3.2b, data on GDP per person from 1870 through 2010 are measured in constant year-1990 dollars adjusted for purchasing power parity and are from the Maddison Project (2013). I extended that series through 2013 by applying the growth rate in GDP per person in constant year-2011 dollars adjusted for purchasing power parity from World Development Indicators (World Bank 2015). I used several different series on government expenditure as a percentage of

GDP from Tanzi (2011) and the Organization for Economic Cooperation and Development (1982, 1992, 2000, 2015e, 2015c), but I was careful only to use data where the different series overlap each other closely in years when both were available. Data on the two variables in figures 3.2a and 3.2b are also available over fairly long periods of time for Ireland and New Zealand, but the Maddison Project data on GDP per person in Ireland has large gaps, while the long-ago historical series on government expenditure in New Zealand from Tanzi (2011) appears to involve significant inconsistencies in the way it was measured when compared to more recent data from New Zealand, based on the fact that the series do not overlap closely in the years when both are available.

21. The 1870–1929 trend is constructed for each country based on a separate regression for each country, in which log real GDP per person is the dependent variable and year is the only explanatory variable.

22. The point that the log of real GDP per person in the United States and many other industrialized countries can be predicted well by extending the trends from the late 1800s through the beginning of the Depression was brought to prominence in economics by Jones (1995). Stokey and Rebelo (1995) cited evidence of this nature about the United States to argue that fundamental tax reform would be highly unlikely to have a significant effect on the long-run economic growth rate in the United States.

23. Another issue is that constructing trends using 1870–1929 data probably understates the pre-Depression trend in log real GDP per person for some countries because these countries were already suffering from recession in the 1920s. Lant Pritchett makes available on his web site (www.hks.harvard.edu/fs/lpritch/EG%20-%20NEW.html) graphs like this for sixteen industrialized countries, with the only difference being that the pre-Depression trend is constructed using the range of years between 1890 and 1929 that yield the best predictions of subsequent growth. When calculated this way, the pre-Depression trends do a remarkably good job of predicting subsequent growth, with a median prediction error for 2003 GDP per person of just 3.9 percent.

24. For further information on the concepts of stationarity and non-stationarity and how to test for them, see any time-series econometric textbook, such as Harris and Solis (2003).

25. To verify that this still holds over the full 1870–2013 period for each of the twenty-three countries depicted in figure 3.5 (excluding Ireland, Luxembourg, and Turkey, which do not have continuous data on GDP per person for the full period), I performed augmented Dickey-Fuller unit root tests on the growth rate in real GDP per person, using a step-down procedure to select the number of lags of first-differenced growth rates (with a maximum of six lags). The tests strongly reject the null hypothesis of non-stationarity for each of the twenty countries, confirming that Jones's point still holds true even with a now considerably longer time series. I also performed a similar test on each country of the null hypothesis that the log of real GDP per person is non-stationary after controlling for a country-specific time trend, and that test failed to reject the null hypothesis of non-stationarity for all of the twenty countries. This means that there is evidence that a country's log real GDP per person can diverge from its long-run historical trend in a permanent way.

26. We cannot perform a formal test of whether government spending as a percentage of GDP has been non-stationary for the full 1870–2013 time period because there are big gaps in data availability before 1960, but we can test for non-stationarity in taxes as a percentage of GDP for twenty-three industrialized countries between the early 1960s through 2013. A similar test to that described in the previous note fails to reject the null hypothesis of non-stationarity for taxes as a percentage of GDP for fourteen of twenty-three industrialized countries and for twenty of twenty-three countries when controlling for a country-specific linear time trend.

27. Romer (1986, 1987, 1990) has made seminal contributions to the theory of endogenous growth.

28. Jones 1995, 496.

29. Due to data availability constraints, both variables are measured for 1920 through 2013 in Ireland and Canada.

30. In all cases throughout this chapter where I say estimates are not statistically significant, they are not significant in their difference

from zero at the 10 percent significance level. In all cases where I say estimates are statistically significant, they are significantly different from zero at the 1 percent significance level. For more precise explanations of regression and statistical significance that should be accessible to people with no background in statistics, see Bakija (2013).

31. The ideas about how capital accumulation and technological change relate to economic growth were brought to prominence in economics by Solow (1957) and Swan (1956). Easterly (2001) offers an accessible and entertaining explanation of leading theories of economic growth, including the ones mentioned here.

32. The slope of the regression line through the scatter plot in the bottom panel of figure 3.3 is identical to the coefficient on change in government spending as a share of GDP in a multiple regression where the dependent variable is the growth rate and the explanatory variables include both change in government spending as a percentage of GDP and initial income. Angrist and Pischke (2009, section 3.1.2) provide a demonstration of why this is so in their discussion of "regression anatomy." See also Bakija (2013) for a less technical demonstration and example.

33. At the average growth rate (2.001 percent per year), real GDP per person after one hundred years would be $1.02001^{100} = 7.252$ times as large in one hundred years as it is initially. Changing the growth rate by the point estimate of the effect of a 10 percent of GDP increase in government spending of -0.078 leads to a real GDP per person that would be 6.72 times as large in one hundred years relative to the initial level, which is about 7 percent smaller than we would have had with the higher growth rate.

34. Fraction of world GDP represented by the thirteen countries in figure 3.3 is my calculation, based on data from the Maddison Project (2013) and Maddison (2010).

35. In figures 3.4a and 3.4b, real GDP per person is measured in constant year 2005 US dollars and is adjusted for purchasing power parity, based on data from the Penn World Tables Version 8.0 (Feenstra, Inklaar, and Timmer 2013) for 1960 through 2011, and extended from 2011 through 2013 by applying the growth rate in real GDP per person in constant year-2011 dollars and adjusted for purchasing power

parity from World Development Indicators (World Bank, 2015). To compute economic growth rates for figure 3.5, I used a similar approach, except that I measured GDP per person in constant local currency units, as recommended by Feenstra, Inklaar, and Timmer (2015). Data on real GDP growth and taxes as a percentage of GDP are also available dating back to the early 1960s for Greece, Luxembourg, Portugal, and Turkey. These are excluded from figures 3.4a and 3.4b to improve their readability, but they are included in figure 3.5. These additional four countries do fit the general patterns of figures 3.4a and 3.4b described in the text. Iceland is excluded due to large gaps in the available data on tax revenue relative to GDP in the earlier years.

36. The point estimate of the slope of the regression line in the bottom panel in figure 3.5 is that a 10 percentage point increase in taxes as a percentage of GDP is associated with an increase in the annual growth rate of real GDP per person of 0.05 percentage points, with a 95 percent confidence interval ranging from -0.3 to +0.4 percentage points. Unfortunately, data on unemployment rates are unavailable for many countries in our sample for the early 1960s. Using the same data as in figure 3.5, a regression of growth rate on change in taxes as a percentage of GDP and initial level of GDP per person, omitting the 2013 unemployment rate, yields a very small and statistically insignificant negative effect of taxes on growth, so the main point emphasized in the text does not actually depend on controlling for the unemployment rate. In that regression, an increase in taxes of 10 percent of GDP, holding initial income constant, is associated with a 0.02 percentage point reduction in the annual growth rate, with a 95 percent confidence interval ranging from -0.4 percentage points to +0.4 percentage points. Krugman (2012) offers a clear and accessible explanation of the most likely causes of the continuing severe recession in the peripheral European countries, which have to do with these countries being tied to the Euro currency at a time when currency devaluation to promote exports would otherwise have been a critical method of boosting their economies in response to the shock of a severe recession, together with being stuck at the zero lower bound for nominal interest rates at a time of weak aggregate demand and very low inflation. Greece, unlike almost all other European countries, also had problems due to

accumulating too much government debt prior to the crisis, but that is as much an issue of tax revenue being too low as it is an issue of high government spending.

37. Slemrod 1995; Myles 2000; Huang and Frentz 2014; Gale and Samwick 2014.

38. Bergh and Henrekson 2011; McBride 2012; Gemmell and Au 2013.

39. See Angrist and Pischke (2009), section 3.2.3, for discussion of "bad control." King (2010) explains the same problem but refers to it as "post-treatment bias."

40. Bergh and Karlsson 2010.

41. Technically, they are estimating a panel regression where the data are collapsed to non-overlapping five-year averages and are controlling for country fixed effects and year fixed effects; the words in the text roughly convey what kind of comparison their evidence is based on.

42. Lindert 2004.

43. Gemmell, Kneller, and Sanz 2011.

44. Gemmell, Kneller, and Sanz (2011) estimate a "single equation error correction model." Enns, Masaki, and Kelly (2014) explain this approach and point out some problems with it.

45. A better way to identify whether there is a long-run equilibrium relationship among variables in time-series data is to work with non-stationary variables and test them for "cointegration," which, roughly speaking, means that the variables tend to return to their long-run equilibrium relationship with each other in the long-run and do not diverge from that relationship in a persistent way. For an introduction to cointegration methods in econometrics, see, for example, Harris and Sollis (2003). In ongoing research (Bakija and Narasimhan 2016), my coauthor and I use panel cointegration techniques on cross-country panel data to test what is essentially the following question: when taxes as a percentage of GDP rise above their historical trend in a persistent way, does that lead log real GDP per person to drop below its historical trend in a persistent way as well, and does that relationship persist over the long run? The results of our panel cointegration tests suggest that the answer to those questions is no.

46. Karras 1999.

47. See, for example, Lindert 2004; Kleinbard 2010; and Kleven 2014.

48. Gemmel, Kneller, and Sanz 2011, F54.

49. Bergh and Karlsson 2010, table 7. In one of the recent literature reviews that argues that taxes do harm economic growth, Bergh and Henrekson (2011, 872) emphasize that they "discuss ... explanations of why several countries with high taxes seem able to enjoy above average growth.... [One] explanation is that countries with large governments compensate for high taxes and spending by implementing market-friendly policies in other areas." They go on to say that this particular explanation is "supported by ongoing research," and they spend much of the latter part of their literature review providing stylized facts to support this conclusion.

50. Chetty 2012.

51. Alesina, Glaeser, and Sacerdote (2005) and Constant and Otterbach (2011) provide further discussion of why individual choice over labor supply might be limited.

52. Prescott 2004a.

53. See, for example, Conard (2012) or Prescott's (2004) own op-ed in the *Wall Street Journal*.

54. Essentially, Prescott assumed a utility function that implied large offsetting substitution and income effects and also assumed that government revenue is given back to people as lump-sum transfers. He then chose the parameters of that utility function to match the observed data. He could have equally well matched the data with a utility function that implied smaller offsetting income and substitution effects and less deadweight loss. See Alesina, Glaeser, and Sacerdote (2005) and Jäntti, Pirttilä, and Selin (2015) for further discussion of these issues.

55. Alesina, Glaeser, and Sacerdote 2005.

56. Gruber and Wise 1999.

57. Data on hours worked are from the Conference Board (2015). Data on population aged fifteen to sixty-four are from World Development Indicators (World Bank 2015). Data on general government tax revenue as a percentage of GDP are from Tanzi (2010) and the Organization

for Economic Cooperation and Development (2015f, 2015c). For a few countries, data on tax as a percentage of GDP is available for 1960 and from 1965 on, but missing for 1961 through 1964. In those cases, I compute the 1960–1969 average of tax as a percentage of GDP by replacing the 1961 through 1964 values with linear interpolations.

58. In the United States, from 2004 to 2013, taxes averaged 25.4 percent of GDP, and hours worked per person aged fifteen to sixty-four averaged 1,243 per year. An increase in taxes of 10 percent of GDP would reduce the net-of-tax share (that is, one minus the tax rate) from 0.746 to 0.646, a 13.4 percent reduction. If that increases annual hours worked per person aged fifteen to sixty-four by 63 hours, that is a 5.07 percent increase in hours worked. 5.07/13.4 is approximately 0.4, which implies a 10 percent increase in after-tax wage would be associated with approximately a 4 percent increase in hours worked.

59. A regression using the annual cross-country panel data for all available years from 1960 through 2013 of the log of average annual hours worked on the log of one minus the tax rate (which is a measure of the incentive to earn income, analogous to the after-tax wage), controlling for country fixed effects and year fixed effects, suggests that a 1 percent increase in the incentive to earn income is associated with a 0.20 percent increase in hours worked, but this is again statistically insignificant, with a wide 95 percent confidence interval ranging from -0.33 to 0.72. Country fixed effects control for any influences on labor supply that differ across countries that are constant over time, and year fixed effects control for any factors that are changing in the same way over time for all countries. I compute robust clustered standard errors with clustering by country, which allows for correlation in the error terms over time within a country. The lack of statistical significance once one controls for country and year fixed effects is consistent with the previous literature—for example, Davis and Henrekson (2005) also found that, in a cross-country panel regression of annual hours worked per adult on the tax rate, statistical significance disappeared when country and year fixed effects were added to the specification.

60. Faggio and Nickell (2007) discuss which European countries had unions that pushed for work-sharing arrangements.

61. Kleven 2014.

62. This is especially counterintuitive given the fact that, when we are talking about participation decisions, both the income and substitution effects of taxes and means-tested transfers ought to go in the direction of less work.

63. Rogerson (2007) and others also made this point previously, but Kleven (2013) brings better data to bear on the question.

64. Jäntti, Pirttilä, and Selin 2015.

65. Jäntti, Pirttilä, and Selin 2015, table 4, column 3. In the regression specification just described, the estimated income effect is close to zero, so the estimated substitution effect, which is what is relevant for determining deadweight loss, is also very close to a 10 percent increase in after-tax wage being associated with a 3 percent increase in hours worked. Among the many specifications Jäntti and his colleagues estimate, there is one that relies exclusively on difference-in-differences variation in after-tax wages across countries for identification. In that specification (table 3, column 4), a 10 percent increase in after-tax wage is associated with a 6.4 percent increase in hours worked. However, this specification also estimates that a 10 percent increase in non-labor income, holding after-tax wage constant, is associated with an *increase* in hours worked of 7 percent, which is implausibly large and the opposite of the expected sign. If both were true at the same time, that would imply a very small substitution effect and thus little deadweight loss from taxation. However, the positive estimated effect of income on hours worked in that specification is most likely due to reverse causality. For example, in the countries where hours worked declined by more for some other reason, it caused non-labor income, such as capital income, to decline because people had less disposable labor income left over to save. This casts that particular regression specification into suspicion. Reverse causality in the estimation of income effects is a pervasive problem in estimating labor supply elasticities. The most credible evidence that we have of income effects on hours worked is from examining how labor earnings respond to randomly winning moderate-sized lottery prizes, and this evidence suggests a very modest elasticity of labor supply with respect to non-labor income of about -0.03, which is much more consistent with the

findings from the Jäntti et al. regression discussed in the text. See Imbens, Rubin, and Sacerdote 2001; and Alesina, Glaeser and Sacerdote 2005, 24.

66. Recent reviews of the literature that send a consistent message about this include Meghir and Phillips 2010; Alesina, Glaeser, and Sacerdote 2005; Chetty 2012; and Chetty et al. 2012. Keane (2011) offers a somewhat contrary view, but see Meghir and Phillips (2010) for a response.

67. Chetty et al. 2012.

68. Chetty 2012.

69. Blomquist and Simula 2012.

70. The 24 percent figure comes from dividing the deadweight loss (0.31) by 1.31.

71. In 2010, the 6 percent of individuals in the United States with annual wage and salary income above $100,000 earned 29 percent of all wage and salary income (this is my calculation, based on Form W2 data available at IRS Tax Stats, which can be viewed at www.irs.gov /file_source/pub/irs-soi/10in02w2.xls). The top 1 percent of the income distribution accounted for about 30 percent of federal government tax revenue in the United States in 2014 (Urban-Brookings Tax Policy Center 2013a). Among US income tax returns with adjusted gross income above $500,000 in 2010, which was somewhat above the threshold to qualify for the top 1 percent in that year, men earned 86 percent of all wage and salary income (this is my calculation, based on Form W2 data available at IRS Tax Stats, which can be viewed at the link given above).

72. Moffitt and Wilhelm 2000.

73. Meghir and Phillips 2010.

74. In figure 3.7, data on real GDP per hour worked are from the Conference Board (2015). Data on educational attainment are from Cohen, Leker, and Soto (2014); see Cohen and Soto (2007) and Cohen and Leker (2014) for further details. Data on taxes as a percentage of GDP are from Tanzi (2011) and OECD (2015a and 2015e).

75. Lindert 2004.

76. Blundell, Bozio, and Laroque 2013.

77. More specifically, economists estimate the percentage change in pre-tax gross income or taxable income that is associated with a 1

percent increase in the "marginal retention rate" (that is, one minus the marginal tax rate). This is known as the "elasticity of taxable income." Saez, Slemrod, and Giertz (2012) provide a comprehensive and critical review of the empirical literature on this subject.

78. It is important to emphasize that the top panel of figure 3.8 shows percentage growth in *pre tax* incomes over time. So the relationship between cuts in marginal income tax rates and income growth shown in the figure is not due to some mechanical relationship where cutting taxes leaves you with more income after taxes. Figure 3.8 is about what happened to incomes measured before taxes got subtracted out.

79. Saez, Slemrod, and Giertz 2012; Weber 2014.

80. See, for example, Feldstein's (2011) article in the *Wall Street Journal*.

81. For a more complete explanation of the various competing theories and citations to the seminal studies on each topic, see, for example, Bakija, Cole, and Heim (2012).

82. See Gordon and Slemrod 2000.

83. Piketty, Saez, and Stantcheva 2014. I update their top income share series using data from the World Top Incomes Database (Alvaredo et al. 2015) and update their marginal tax rate series using data from the Organization for Economic Cooperation and Development (2015a). Growth rates in the bottom panel of figure 3.9 are based on real GDP per person in constant local currency units from the Penn World Tables Version 8.0 (Feenstra, Inklaar, and Timmer 2015), extended from 2011 through 2013 by applying the growth rate in real GDP per person in constant local currency units from World Development Indicators (World Bank 2015).

84. Using the data in the top panel of figure 3.9, I estimate a regression of the change in the log of the top 1 percent income share against the change in the log of the retention rate. The coefficient on the log retention rate, which is the estimate of the elasticity of taxable income, is 0.469, with a 95 percent confidence interval ranging from 0.202 to 0.734. This is roughly similar to the elasticity of taxable income that Piketty, Saez, and Stantcheva (2014) estimated using similar data but a somewhat different approach.

85. Here, I translate what Piketty, Saez, and Stantcheva (2014) estimated into what they imply about revenue-maximizing tax rate and deadweight loss based on an analysis in Giertz (2009).

86. $1.59 / (1.59 + 1) = 61$ percent.

87. In their article, Piketty, Saez, and Stantcheva (2014) also show that the lack of a statistically significant correlation between change in top tax rates and economic growth persists after controlling for initial GDP per person, among other things, and I've verified that this is still true by estimating similar regressions on the updated data used here.

88. To corroborate this point, Piketty, Saez, and Stantcheva (2014) show that a significant portion of executive pay rewards luck. For example, stock options reward executives for market-wide increases in stock market valuations as opposed to the relative performance of the executive's firm compared to the stock market as a whole. Compensation for luck should not be part of an optimal incentive pay scheme for executives. Piketty and his coauthors then show that the portion of pay that rewards luck is higher during periods of recent US history when top marginal tax rates were lower.

89. Bakija, Cole, and Heim 2012.

90. In 2009, there were only about 5,000 publicly traded firms in the United States, compared to about 150,000 tax units in the top 0.1 percent of the income distribution (Stuart 2011; Piketty and Saez 2003. Piketty and Saez updated their tables and figures in 2015, and the updated information can be viewed at http://eml.berkeley.edu//~saez /TabFig2014prel.xls). However, large publicly traded firms could have large numbers of executives and managers represented in the top 0.1 percent.

91. For accessible, interesting, and provocative discussions of these issues by leading financial economists, see Zingales 2015; Malkiel 2013; Greenwood and Scharfstein 2013; and Cochrane 2013.

92. Cutler (2014, ch. 2) offers an accessible discussion of evidence on this topic.

93. Murphy, Shleifer, and Vishny (1991) discuss various ways in which the legal profession might be involved in rent-seeking, and they demonstrate a cross-country correlation between the proportion of college students who go into law and slower economic growth.

94. See Saez, Slemrod, and Giertz's (2012) discussion of "fiscal externalities" for an explanation of why, if estimated elasticities of taxable income reflect shifting of reported income between the corporate and personal tax base, the implied deadweight loss per dollar of revenue raised by a tax increase is smaller. Part of the explanation is that, if we increase the personal income tax rate and some of the reduction in personal taxable income represents shifting of income to the corporate tax base, then decline in personal income tax revenue is partly offset by an increase in corporate tax revenue, so that deadweight loss per dollar of overall government revenue raised is much smaller than we'd infer when we just look at the personal income tax in isolation.

95. Giertz 2009.

96. 0.33 / (1 + 0.33) = 24.8 percent. Ideally, we ought to also take into account the marginal change in compliance and administrative costs in this calculation. In our book, *Taxing Ourselves* (Slemrod and Bakija 2016), my coauthor and I show that estimates of the *average* administrative and compliance costs of the US tax system are on the order of 10 to 15 percent of revenue raised. However, *marginal* administrative and compliance costs (that is, how such costs *change* when we raise the top marginal tax rate) are what matter here, and these could be much lower than the average cost, since many compliance and administrative costs are fixed relative to the marginal tax rate. In other words, raising the income tax rate in the top bracket by 1 percentage point is unlikely to have much effect on the overall costs to the taxpayer of complying with the tax code or the costs to the IRS of collecting the revenue.

97. Diamond and Saez (2011) argue for much higher tax rates on high-income taxpayers in the United States on these grounds.

4. THINKING SENSIBLY ABOUT THE SIZE OF GOVERNMENT

1. See chapter 1; and Madrick 2009.

2. This includes all levels of government: federal, state, and local.

3. Libertarians regard most government programs, other than those protecting safety and property rights, as illegitimate infringements on

individual freedom. However, very few Americans are libertarians. Most of us believe that decisions about where and how government acts should be determined mainly by whether such action makes things better.

4. For details, evidence, and references, see chapters 1–3.

5. Pew Research Center 2012.

6. See Kenworthy 2014, ch. 5.

REFERENCES

Aaron, Henry. 2013. "Progressives and the Safety Net." *Democracy*, Winter: 68–79.

Aaronson, Daniel, and Bhashkar Mazumder. 2008. "Intergenerational Economic Mobility in the U.S., 1940 to 2000." *Journal of Human Resources* 43: 139–172.

Acs, Gregory, Pamela J. Loprest, and Austin Nichols. 2009. "Risk and Recovery: Documenting the Changing Risks to Family Incomes." Urban Institute. www.urban.org/research/publication/risk-and-recovery-documenting-changing-risks-family-incomes.

Adema, Willem, Pauline Fron, and Maxime Ladaique. 2014. "How Much Do OECD Countries Spend on Social Protection and How Redistributive Are Their Tax/Benefit Systems?" *International Social Security Review* 67: 1–25.

Agell, Jonas, Henry Ohlsson, and Peter Skogman Thoursie. 2006. "Growth Effects of Government Expenditure and Taxation in Rich Countries: A Comment." *European Economic Review* 50: 211–218.

Alesina, Alberto, Edward Glaeser, and Bruce Sacerdote. 2005. "Work and Leisure in the U.S. and Europe: Why So Different?" *NBER Macroeconomics Annual* 20 (1): 1–64.

Allard, Gayle J., and Peter H. Lindert. 2007. "Euro-Productivity and Euro-Jobs since the 1960s: Which Institutions Really Mattered?" In

The New Comparative Economic History: Essays in Honor of Jeffrey G. Williamson, edited by Timothy J. Hatton, Kevin H. O'Rourke, and Alan M. Taylor, 365–394. Cambridge, MA: MIT Press.

Altonji, Joseph G., and Richard K. Mansfield. 2011. "The Role of Family, School, and Community Characteristics in Inequality in Education and Labor-Market Outcomes." In *Whither Opportunity? Rising Inequality, Schools, and Children's Life Chances*, edited by Greg J. Duncan and Richard J. Murnane, 339–358. New York: Russell Sage Foundation.

Alvaredo, Facundo, Anthony B. Atkinson, Thomas Piketty, and Emmanuel Saez. 2015. "The World Wealth and Income Database." Accessed April 3, 2015. www.wid.world.

American Society of Civil Engineers. 2013. "Report Card for America's Infrastructure." www.infrastructurereportcard.org.

Anderson, Monica, and Andrew Perrin. 2015. "15% of Americans Don't Use the Internet. Who Are They?" Pew Research Center. www.pewresearch.org/fact-tank/2015/07/28/15-of-americans-dont-use-the-internet-who-are-they.

Angrist, Joshua D., and Jörn-Steffen Pischke. 2009. *Mostly Harmless Econometrics: An Empiricist's Companion.* Princeton, NJ: Princeton University Press.

Anrig, Greg, Jr. 2006. "Creating a Softer Economic Cushion." The Century Foundation.

Arneson, Richard. 2012. "Justice." In *The Oxford Handbook of Political Philosophy*, edited by David Estlund, 58–75. Oxford: Oxford University Press.

Arum, Richard, and Josipa Roksa. 2011. *Academically Adrift: Limited Learning on College Campuses.* Chicago: University of Chicago Press.

Atkinson, Anthony B. 1999. *The Economic Consequences of Rolling Back the Welfare State.* Cambridge, MA: MIT Press.

Autor, David H. 2010. "The Polarization of Job Opportunities in the U.S. Labor Market." Center for American Progress and the Hamilton Project. www.brookings.edu/research/papers/2010/04/jobs-autor.

Avent, Ryan. 2011. *The Gated City.* Amazon Digital Services.

Bailey, Martha, and Susan Dynarski. 2011. "Gains and Gaps: A Historical Perspective on Inequality in College Entry and Completion." In *Whither Opportunity? Rising Inequality, Schools, and Children's Life Chances,* edited by Greg J. Duncan and Richard J. Murnane, 117–131. New York: Russell Sage Foundation.

Baker, Dean. 2011. *The End of Loser Liberalism.* Washington, DC: Center for Economic and Policy Research.

Baker, Tom, and David Moss. 2009. "Government as Risk Manager." In *New Perspectives on Regulation,* edited by David Moss and John Cisternino, 87–109. Cambridge, MA: The Tobin Project.

Bakija, Jon. 2013. "A Non-Technical Introduction to Regression." Working paper, Williams College. web.williams.edu/Economics /wp/Bakija-Non-Technical-Introduction-to-Regression.pdf.

Bakija, Jon, Adam Cole, and Brad Heim. 2012. "Jobs and Income Growth of Top Earners and the Causes of Changing Income Inequality: Evidence from U.S. Tax Return Data." Working paper, Williams College. web.williams.edu/Economics/wp/BakijaColeHeimJobs IncomeGrowthTopEarners.pdf.

Bakija, Jon, and Tarun Narasimhan. 2016. "Effects of the Level and Structure of Taxes on Long-Run Economic Growth: What Can We Learn from Panel Time-Series Techniques?" Working paper, Williams College. web.williams.edu/Economics/wp/Bakija NarasimhanTaxEconomicGrowthPanelTimeSeries.pdf.

Barnett, W. Steven, Megan E. Carolan, Jen Fitzgerald, and James H. Squires. 2011. "The State of Preschool 2011." National Institute for Early Education Research. nieer.org/sites/nieer/files/2011yearbook .pdf

Ben-Galim, D., and A. Sachraida Dal, eds. 2009. *Now It's Personal: Learning from Welfare-to-Work Approaches Around the World.* Washington, DC: Institute for Public Policy Research.

Bergh, Andreas, and Magnus Henrekson. 2011. "Government Size and Growth: A Survey and Interpretation of the Evidence." *Journal of Economic Surveys* 25 (5): 872–897.

Bergh, Andreas, and Martin Karlsson. 2010. "Government Size and Growth: Accounting for Economic Freedom and Globalization." *Public Choice* 142 (1–2): 195–213.

Blau, Francine. 2012. *The Economics of Women, Men, and Work*. 6th ed. Englewood Cliffs, NJ: Prentice-Hall.

Blinder, Alan S. 2009. "How Many U.S. Jobs Might Be Offshorable?" *World Economics* 10 (2): 41–78.

Blomquist, Soren, and Laurent Simula. 2012. "Marginal Deadweight Loss When the Income Tax is Nonlinear." www.vanderbilt.edu /econ/conference/taxation-theory/documents/Blomquist-Simula .pdf.

Bloome, Deirdre, and Bruce Western. 2011. "Cohort Change and Racial Differences in Educational and Income Mobility." *Social Forces* 90: 375–395.

Blundell, Richard, Antoine Bozio, and Guy Laroque. 2013. "Extensive and Intensive Margins of Labour Supply: Work and Working Hours in The US, UK And France." *Fiscal Studies* 34 (1): 1–29.

Bolt, Jutta, and Jan Luiten van Zanden. 2014. "The Maddison Project: Collaborative Research on Historical National Accounts." *The Economic History Review* 67 (3): 627–651.

Bourgin, Frank. 1989. *The Great Challenge: The Myth of Laissez-Faire in the Early Republic*. New York: Harper and Row.

Bowen, William G., Matthew M. Chingos, and Michael S. McPherson. 2009. *Crossing the Finish Line: Completing College at America's Public Universities*. Princeton, NJ: Princeton University Press.

Bureau of Labor Statistics. 2015. "Selected Paid Leave Benefits." www .bls.gov/news.release/ebs2.to6.htm.

Burnstein, Daniel. 2006. *Next to Godliness: Confronting Dirt and Despair in the Progressive Era* Urbana: University of Illinois Press.

Butts, R. Freeman. 1978. *Public Education in the United States from Revolution to Reform*. New York: Holt Rinehart and Winston.

Carneiro, Pedro, and James Heckman. 2003. "Human Capital Policy." In *Inequality in America: What Role for Human Capital Policies?*, edited by James Heckman and Anne Krueger, 77–239. Cambridge, MA: MIT Press.

Carpenter, Dick M., Lisa Knepper, Angela E. Erickson, and John K. Ross. 2012. *License to Work: A National Study of the Burdens from Occupational Licensing*. Arlington, VA: Institute for Justice.

Castles, Francis G., Stephan Leibfried, Jane Lewis, Herbert Obinger, and Christopher Pierson, eds. 2010. *The Oxford Handbook of the Welfare State*. Oxford: Oxford University Press.

Center for Retirement Security. 2009. "Workers with Pension Coverage, by Pension Type, 1983, 1995, and 2007."

Center on Budget and Policy Priorities. 2015. "Where do Our Federal Tax Dollars Go?" March 11. Accessed May 26, 2015. www.cbpp.org /sites/default/files/atoms/files/4-14-08tax.pdf.

Cherlin, Andrew. 2009. *The Marriage-Go-Round*. New York: Knopf.

Chetty, Raj. 2012. "Bounds on Elasticities with Optimization Frictions: A Synthesis of Micro and Macro Evidence on Labor Supply." *Econometrica* 80 (3): 968–1018.

Chetty, Raj, Adam Guren, Day Manoli, and Andrea Weber. 2012. "Does Indivisible Labor Explain the Difference Between Micro and Macro Elasticities? A Meta-Analysis of Extensive Margin Elasticities." *NBER Macroeconomics Annual* 27 (1): 1–56. dx.doi .org/10.1086/669170.

Cochrane, John H. 2013. "Finance: Function Matters, Not Size." *Journal of Economic Perspectives* 27 (2): 29–50.

Cohen, Daniel, and Laura Leker, 2014. "Health and Education: Another Look with the Proper Data." Working paper, Paris School of Economics. Accessed April 24, 2014. www.parisschoolofeconomics .eu/docs/cohen-daniel/cohen-leker-health-and-education-2014.pdf.

Cohen, Daniel, Laura Leker, and Marcelo Soto. 2014. "International Educational Attainment Database." Accessed April 24, 2014. www .parisschoolofeconomics.eu/en/cohen-daniel/ international-educational-attainment-database/.

Cohen, Daniel, and Marcelo Soto. 2007. "Growth and Human Capital: Good Data, Good Results." *Journal of Economic Growth* 12: 51–76.

Conard, Edward. 2012. *Unintended Consequences: Why Everything You've Been Told About the Economy is Wrong*. New York: Portfolio /Penguin.

Conference Board. 2015. *The Conference Board Total Economy Database™: May 2015*. Accessed June 9, 2015. www.conference-board.org/data /economydatabase/.

Congressional Budget Office. 2008. "Recent Trends in the Variability of Individual Earnings and Household Income." www.cbo.gov /publication/41714.

———. 2011. "Estimated Impact of the American Recovery and Reinvestment Act on Employment and Economic Output."

———. 2013. "The Distribution of Federal Spending and Taxes in 2006." November 7. Accessed April 25, 2015. www.cbo.gov/sites /default/files/44698-Distribution_11–2013.pdf.

Constant, Amelie F., and Steffen Otterbach. 2011. "Work Hours Constraints: Impacts and Policy Implications." December. IZA Policy Paper No. 35. Accessed May 29, 2015. ftp.iza.org/pp35.pdf.

Cooper, Donna. 2012. "Meeting the Infrastructure Imperative." Center for American Progress. www.americanprogress.org/issues /general/report/2012/02/16/11068/meeting-the-infrastructure-imperative.

Cooper, Kerris, and Kitty Stewart. 2013. "Does Money Affect Children's Outcomes? A Systematic Review." Joseph Rowntree Foundation. www.jrf.org.uk/report/does-money-affect-children%E2%80%99s-outcomes.

Cox, W. Michael, and Richard Alm. 1999. *Myths of Rich and Poor.* New York: Basic Books.

Currie, Janet. 2011. "Inequality at Birth: Some Causes and Consequences." *American Economic Review* 101 (3): 1–22.

Cutler, David. 2014. *The Quality Cure: How Focusing on Health Care Quality Can Save Your Life and Lower Spending Too.* Berkeley: University of California Press.

Cutler, David M., and Dan P. Ly. 2011. "The (Paper)Work of Medicine: Understanding International Medical Costs." *Journal of Economic Perspectives* 25 (2): 3–25.

Dahlberg, Matz, Karin Edmark, and Heléne Lundqvist. 2011. "Ethnic Diversity and Preferences for Redistribution." IFN Working Paper 860, Research Institute of Industrial Economics, Stockholm. www .ifn.se/wfiles/wp/wp860.pdf.

Dalgaard, Carl-Johan, and Claus Thustrup Kreiner. 2003. "Endogenous Growth: A Knife Edge or the Razor's Edge?" *Scandinavian Journal of Economics* 105: 73–85.

Davis, Steven J., and Magnus Henrekson. 2005. "Tax Effects on Work Activity, Industry Mix and Shadow Economy Size: Evidence from Rich Country Comparisons." In *Labour Supply and Incentives to Work in Europe*, edited by Ramon Gomez-Salvador, Ana Lamo, Barbara Petrongolo, Melanie Ward, and Etienne Wasmer, 44–104. Cheltenham, UK: Edward Elgar.

Davis, Karen, Cathy Schoen, and Kristof Stremikis. 2010. "Mirror, Mirror on the Wall: How the Performance of the U.S. Health Care System Compares Internationally." Commonwealth Fund. www .commonwealthfund.org/publications/fund-reports/2010/jun/mirror-mirror-update.

DeLong, J. Bradford. 2009. "Slow Income Growth and Absolute Poverty in the North Atlantic Region." Working paper, University of California, Berkeley.

DeParle, Jason. 2004. *American Dream*. New York: Penguin.

———. 2012. "Welfare Limits Left Poor Adrift as Recession Took Hold." *New York Times*, April 7.

Diamond, Peter A., and Peter Orszag. 2004. *Saving Social Security: A Balanced Approach*. Washington, DC: Brookings Institution Press.

Diamond, Peter, and Emmanuel Saez. 2011. "The Case for a Progressive Tax: From Basic Research to Policy Recommendations." *Journal of Economic Perspectives* 25 (4): 165–190.

Duncan, Greg J., and Jeanne Brooks-Gunn, eds. 1999. *Consequences of Growing Up Poor*. New York: Russell Sage Foundation.

Duncan, Greg J., and Richard J. Murnane, eds. 2011. *Whither Opportunity? Rising Inequality, Schools, and Children's Life Chances*. New York: Russell Sage Foundation.

Duncan, Greg J., Kathleen M. Ziol-Guest, and Ariel Kalil. 2010. "Early-Childhood Poverty and Adult Attainment, Behavior, and Health." *Child Development* 81: 306–325.

Dworkin, Ronald. 2000. *Sovereign Virtue: The Theory and Practice of Equality*. Cambridge, MA: Harvard University Press.

Dynan, Karen. 2010. "The Income Rollercoaster: Rising Income Volatility and Its Implications." *Pathways*, Spring: 3–6.

Dynan, Karen E., Douglas W. Elmendorf, and Daniel E. Sichel. 2012. "The Evolution of Household Income Volatility." *B.E. Journal of*

Economic Analysis and Policy 12. www.degruyter.com/view/j/bejeap
.2012.12.issue-2/1935-1682.3347/1935-1682.3347.xml.

Dynarski, Susan, and Judith Scott-Clayton. 2013. "Financial Aid Policy: Lessons from Research." NBER Working Paper 18710, National Bureau of Economic Research.

Easterly, William. 2001. *The Elusive Quest for Growth*. Cambridge, MA: MIT Press

Eberstadt, Nicholas. 2008. "The Poverty of the Official Poverty Rate." AmericanEnterpriseInstitute.www.aei.org/publication/the-poverty-of-the-official-poverty-rate.

Economic Mobility Project. 2012. "Pursuing the American Dream: Economic Mobility Across Generations." Pew Charitable Trusts. www
.pewtrusts.org/~/media/legacy/uploadedfiles/wwwpewtrustsorg
/reports/economic_mobility/pursuingamericandreampdf.pdf.

Economist. 2008. "The Trouble with Pensions." June 12.

Edin, Kathryn, and Laura Lein. 1997. *Making Ends Meet*. New York: Russell Sage Foundation.

Edin, Kathryn, and H. Luke Schaefer. 2015. *$2 a Day: Living on Almost Nothing in America*. Boston: Houghton Mifflin Harcourt.

Eggleston, Karen N., and Victor R. Fuchs. 2012. "The New Demographic Transition: Most Gains in Life Expectancy Now Realized Late in Life." *Journal of Economic Perspectives* 26 (3): 137–156.

Ehrenreich, Barbara. 2001. *Nickel and Dimed: On (Not) Getting By in America*. New York: Henry Holt and Company.

Ellwood, David T., and Christopher Jencks. 2004. "The Uneven Spread of Single-Parent Families: What Do We Know? Where Do We Look for Answers?" In *Social Inequality*, edited by Kathryn M. Neckerman, 3–77. New York: Russell Sage Foundation.

Enns, Peter K., Takaaki Masaki, and Nathan J. Kelly. 2014. "Time-Series Analysis and Spurious Regression: An Error Correction." Working paper, Cornell University. Accessed January 1, 2016. takaakimasaki.com/wp-content/uploads/2014/08/EnnsMasakiKelly_ECM_9.25.14.pdf.

Ermisch, John, Markus Jäntti, and Timothy Smeeding, eds. 2012. *From Parents to Children: The Intergenerational Transmission of Advantage*. New York: Russell Sage Foundation.

Esping-Andersen, Gøsta. 2004. "Unequal Opportunities and the Mechanisms of Social Inheritance." In *Generational Income Mobility in North America and Europe,* edited by Miles Corak, 289–314. Cambridge, UK: Cambridge University Press.

———. 2009. *The Incomplete Revolution.* Cambridge, UK: Polity.

———. 2011. "The Social Democratic Road to Equality." Working paper, Universitat Pompeu Fabra.

Esping-Andersen, Gøsta, and Sandra Wagner. 2012. "Asymmetries in the Opportunity Structure: Intergenerational Mobility Trends in Europe." *Research in Social Stratification and Mobility* 30: 473–487.

Faggio, Giulia, and Stephen Nickell. 2007. "Patterns of Work across the OECD." *Economic Journal* 117 (521): 416–440.

Federal Communications Commission. 2015. "Internet Access Services Report."

Federal Highway Administration. 2014. "Deficient Bridges by State and Highway System." www.fhwa.dot.gov/bridge/deficient .cfm.

Feenstra, Robert C., Robert Inklaar, and Marcel P. Timmer. 2015. "The Next Generation of the Penn World Table." *American Economic Review* 105: 3150–3182. www.ggdc.net/pwt.

Feldstein, Martin. 2011. "The Tax Reform Evidence from 1986." *Wall Street Journal,* October 24. www.wsj.com/articles/SB10001424052970 2040023045766294815717778262.

Ferrarini, Tommy, and Ann-Zofie Duvander. 2010. "Earner-Carer Model at the Cross-Roads: Reforms and Outcomes of Sweden's Family Policy in Comparative Perspective." *International Journal of Health Services* 40: 373–398.

Fischer, Claude S. 2010. *Made in America.* Chicago: University of Chicago Press.

Fischer, Claude S., Michael Hout, Martin Sanchez Jankowski, Samuel R. Lucas, Ann Swidler, and Kim Voss. 1996. *Inequality by Design.* Princeton, NJ: Princeton University Press.

Fishback, Price, Robert Higgs, Gary D. Libecap, John Joseph Wallis, Stanley L. Engerman, Jeffrey Rogers Hummel, Sumner J. La Croix, et al. 2007. *Government and the American Economy: A New History.* Chicago: University of Chicago Press.

Flanagan, Robert J. 1988. "Unemployment as a Hiring Problem." *OECD Economic Studies,* 11 (autumn): 123–154.

———. 1999. "Macroeconomic Performance and Collective Bargaining: An International Perspective." *Journal of Economic Literature* 37 (3): 1150–1175.

Fletcher, Michael A. 2013. "401(k) Breaches Undermining Retirement Security for Millions." *Washington Post,* January 15.

Folster, Stefan, and Magnus Henrekson. 2001. "Growth Effects of Government Expenditure and Taxation in Rich Countries." *European Economic Review* 45: 1501–1520.

Frank, Robert, and Ben Bernanke. 2013. *Principles of Macroeconomics.* 5th ed. New York: McGraw-Hill.

Freeman, Richard B., and Peter Gottschalk, eds. 1998. *Generating Jobs: How to Increase Demand for Less-Skilled Workers.* New York: Russell Sage Foundation.

Frick, Walter. 2015. "Welfare Makes America More Entrepreneurial." *Atlantic,* March 26. www.theatlantic.com/politics/archive/2015/03/welfare-makes-america-more-entrepreneurial/388598/.

Friedman, Milton. 1962. *Capitalism and Freedom.* Chicago: University of Chicago Press.

Furman, Jason. 2015. "Smart Social Programs." *New York Times,* May 11.

Gadanne, Lucie, and Monica Singhal. 2014. "Decentralization in Developing Economies." *Annual Review of Economics* 6: 581–604.

Gale, William G., and Andrew A. Samwick. 2014. "Effects of Income Tax Changes on Economic Growth." September. Working paper, Economic Studies at Brookings. www.brookings.edu/~/media/research/files/papers/2014/09/09-effects-income-tax-changes-economic-growth-gale-samwick/09_effects_income_tax_changes_economic_growth_gale_samwick.pdf.

Garfinkel, Irwin, Lee Rainwater, and Timothy M. Smeeding. 2010. *Wealth and Welfare States: Is America a Laggard Or Leader?* Oxford: Oxford University Press.

Gemmell, Norman, and Joey Au. 2013. "Do Smaller Governments Raise the Level or Growth of Output? A Review of Recent Evidence." *Review of Economics* 64: 85–116.

Gemmell, Norman, Richard Kneller, and Ismael Sanz. 2011. "The Timing and Persistence of Fiscal Policy Impacts on Growth: Evidence from OECD Countries." *The Economic Journal* 212 (February): F33–F58.

Ghilarducci, Teresa. 2008. *When I'm Sixty-Four.* Princeton, NJ: Princeton University Press.

Giertz, Seth H. 2009. "The Elasticity of Taxable Income: Influences on Economic Efficiency and Tax Revenues, and Implications for Tax Policy." In *Tax Policy Lessons from the 2000s,* edited by Alan D. Viard, 101–136. Washington, DC: AEI Press.

Glaeser, Edward. 2011. *Triumph of the City.* New York: Penguin.

Gordon, Roger, and Wei Li. 2009. "Tax Structures in Developing Countries: Many Puzzles and a Possible Explanation." *Journal of Public Economics* 93 (7–8): 855–866.

Gordon, Roger, and Joel Slemrod. 2000. "Are 'Real' Responses to Taxes Simply Income Shifting between Corporate and Personal Tax Bases?" In *Does Atlas Shrug? The Economic Consequences of Taxing the Rich,* edited by Joel Slemrod, 240–280. Cambridge, MA: Harvard University Press.

Gornick, Janet C., and Marcia K. Meyers. 2003. *Families That Work.* New York: Russell Sage Foundation.

Gosselin, Peter, and Seth Zimmerman. 2008. "Trends in Income Volatility and Risk, 1970–2004." Urban Institute. www.urban.org /research/publication/trends-income-volatility-and-risk-1970– 2004.

Graetz, Michael J., and Jerry L. Mashaw. 1999. *True Security: Rethinking American Social Insurance.* New Haven, CT: Yale University Press.

Greenwood, Robin, and David Scharfstein. 2013. "The Growth of Finance." *Journal of Economic Perspectives* 27 (2): 3–28.

Gruber, Jonathan. 2013. *Public Finance and Public Policy.* 4th ed. New York: Worth Publishers.

Gruber, Jonathan, and David A. Wise. 1999. "Introduction to Social Security and Retirement around the World." In *Social Security and Retirement around the World,* edited by Jonathan Gruber and David A. Wise, 1–35. Chicago: University of Chicago Press.

Hacker, Jacob S., and Elizabeth Jacobs. 2008. "The Rising Instability of American Family Incomes, 1969–2004." Economic Policy Institute. epi.org/publication/bp213.

Harding, David J., Christopher Jencks, Leonard M. Lopoo, and Susan E. Mayer. 2005. "The Changing Effect of Family Background on the Incomes of American Adults." In *Unequal Chances: Family Background and Economic Success,* edited by Samuel Bowles, Herbert Gintis, and Melissa Osborne Groves, 100–144. New York: Russell Sage Foundation.

Harris, Richard, and Robert Sollis. 2003. *Applied Time Series Modelling and Forecasting.* West Sussex: John Wiley and Sons.

Hauser, Robert M., John Robert Warren, Min-Hsiung Huang, and Wendy Y. Carter. 2000. "Occupational Status, Education, and Social Mobility in the Meritocracy." In *Meritocracy and Economic Inequality,* edited by Kenneth Arrow, Samuel Bowles, and Steven Durlauf, 179–229. Princeton, NJ: Princeton University Press.

Hausmann, Ricardo, Lant Pritchett, and Dani Rodrik. 2005. "Growth Accelerations." *Journal of Economic Growth* 10: 303–329.

Hays, Sharon. 2003. *Flat Broke with Children.* Oxford: Oxford University Press.

Heckman, James J. 2008. "Schools, Skills, and Synapses." NBER Working Paper 14064, National Bureau of Economic Research.

———. 2012. "Promoting Social Mobility." *Boston Review,* September /October. www.bostonreview.net/forum/promoting-social-mobility-james-heckman.

Heston, Alan, Robert Summers, and Bettina Aten. 2012. "Penn World Table Version 7.1." November. Center for International Comparisons of Production, Income and Prices at the University of Pennsylvania. www.rug.nl/research/ggdc/data/pwt/pwt-7.1.

Heymann, Jody, Hye Jin Rho, John Schmitt, and Alison Earle. 2009. "Contagion Nation: A Comparison of Sick Leave Policies in 22 Countries." Center for Economic Development Research. cepr.net /publications/reports/contagion-nation.

Hout, Michael. 2009. "Rationing College Opportunity." *American Prospect,* November: A8–A10.

Huang, Chye-Ching, and Nathaniel Frentz. 2014. "What *Really* is the Evidence on Taxes and Growth?" Washington, DC: Center on Budget and Policy Priorities. www.cbpp.org/sites/default/files /atoms/files/2–18–14tax.pdf.

Imbens, Guido W., Donald B. Rubin, and Bruce I. Sacerdote. 2001. "Estimating the Effect of Unearned Income on Labor Earnings, Savings, and Consumption: Evidence from a Survey of Lottery Players." *American Economic Review* 91: 778–794.

Institution for Social and Policy Studies. 2013. "Economic Security Index." www.economicsecurityindex.org.

Internal Revenue Service, Statistics of Income Division. 2014. "SOI Tax Stats: Historical Table 23." Accessed March 24, 2015. www.irs .gov/uac/SOI-Tax-Stats-Historical-Table-23.

International Centre for Tax and Development. 2015. "The ICTD Government Revenue Dataset." Accessed August 17, 2015. www .ictd.ac/dataset.

Jacob, Brian, and Jens Ludwig. 2008 "Improving Educational Outcomes for Poor Children." NBER Working Paper 14550, National Bureau of Economic Research.

Jäntti, Markus, Jukka Pirttilä, and Håkan Selin. 2015. "Estimating Labour Supply Elasticities Based on Cross-Country Micro Data: A Bridge between Micro and Macro Estimates?" *Journal of Public Economics* 127: 87–99. dx.doi.org/10.1016/j.jpubeco.2014.12.006.

Jencks, Christopher. 2009. "The Graduation Gap." *The American Prospect*, November: A5–A7.

Jencks, Christopher, and Susan Mayer. 1990. "The Social Consequences of Growing Up in a Poor Neighborhood." In *Inner-City Poverty in the United States*, edited by Laurence Lynn and Michael McGeary, 111–186. Washington, DC: National Academy Press.

Jensen, Shane T., and Stephen H. Shore. 2008. "Changes in the Distribution of Income Volatility." Unpublished paper. arxiv.org /pdf/0808.1090.pdf.

Jones, Charles I. 1995. "Time Series Tests of Endogenous Growth Models." *Quarterly Journal of Economics* 110: 495–525.

Joshi, Heather, and Pierella Paci, with Gerald Makepeace and Jane Waldfogel. 1998. *Unequal Pay for Women and Men: Evidence from the British Birth Cohort Studies.* Cambridge, MA: MIT Press.

Kanter, Rosabeth Moss. 2015. *Move: Putting America's Infrastructure Back in the Lead.* New York: W. W. Norton.

Kaplow, Louis. 2008. *The Theory of Taxation and Public Economics.* Princeton, NJ: Princeton University Press.

Karras, Georgios. 1999. "Taxes and Growth: Testing the Neoclassical and Endogenous Growth Models." *Contemporary Economic Policy* 17: 177–188.

Kato, Junko. 2003. *Regressive Taxation and the Welfare State: Path Dependence and Policy Diffusion.* Cambridge, UK: Cambridge University Press.

Kaushal, Neeraj, Katherine Magnuson, and Jane Waldfogel. 2011. "How Is Family Income Related to Investments in Children's Learning?" In *Whither Opportunity? Rising Inequality, Schools, and Children's Life Chances,* edited by Greg J. Duncan and Richard J. Murnane, 187–205. New York: Russell Sage Foundation.

Keane, Michael P. 2011. "Labor Supply and Taxes: A Survey." *Journal of Economic Literature* 49: 961–1075.

Kenworthy, Lane. 2008. *Jobs with Equality.* Oxford: Oxford University Press.

———. 2011. *Progress for the Poor.* Oxford: Oxford University Press.

———. 2013. "What's Wrong with Predistribution?" *Juncture* 20: 111–117.

———. 2014. *Social Democratic America.* New York: Oxford University Press.

———. 2015. "Do Employment-Conditional Earnings Subsidies Work?" ImPRovE Working Paper 15-10, Herman Deleeck Centre for Social Policy, University of Antwerp. improve-research.eu/?wp dmact=process&did=ODcuaG9obGluaw==.

———. 2016a. "A Decent and Rising Income Floor." wp.me /P8wob-2vH.

———. 2016b. "Enabling Social Policy." In *The Uses of Social Investment,* edited by Anton Hemerijck. Oxford: Oxford University Press.

———. 2016c. "Equality of Opportunity." wp.me/P8wob-2lV.

———. 2016d. "Public Insurance and the Least Well-Off." wp.me /P8wob-2xN.

———. 2016e. "Shared Prosperity." wp.me/P8wob-2Dx.

———. 2016f. "Stable Income and Expenses." wp.me/P8wob-2C2.

King, Gary. 2010. "A Hard Unsolved Problem? Post-Treatment Bias in Big Social Science Questions." Slides from a talk given at Harvard University, April 10. Accessed May 29, 2015. gking.harvard.edu /files/gking/files/bigprobP.pdf.

Klein, Ezra. 2007. "The Health of Nations." *American Prospect,* May: 17–21.

Kleinbard, Edward. 2010. "An American Dual Income Tax: Nordic Precedents." *Northwestern Journal of Law and Social Policy* 5: 39–86.

Kletzer, Lori G., and Robert E. Litan. 2001. "A Prescription to Relieve Worker Anxiety." Policy Brief 01-2, Peterson Institute for International Economics. www.iie.com/publications/pb/pb.cfm?ResearchID=70.

Kleven, Henrik Jacobsen. 2014. "How Can Scandinavians Tax So Much?" *Journal of Economic Perspectives* 28 (4): 77–98.

Knoller, Richard, Michael Bleaney, and Norman Gemmell. 1999. "Fiscal Policy and Growth: Evidence from OECD Countries." *Journal of Public Economics* 74: 171–190.

Knuse, Agneta. 2010. "A Stable Pension System: The Eighth Wonder." In *Population Ageing: A Threat to the Welfare State?,* edited by Tommy Bengtsson, 47–64. Berlin: Springer-Verlag.

Kornrich, Sabino, and Frank Furstenberg. 2013. "Investing in Children: Changes in Spending on Children, 1972 to 2007." *Demography* 50: 1–23.

Kotlikoff, Laurence J., and Christian Hagist. 2005. "Who's Going Broke? Comparing Healthcare Costs in Ten OECD Countries." NBER Working Paper 11833, National Bureau of Economic Research.

Krugman, Paul. 2012. *End This Depression Now.* New York: W.W. Norton.

Kulikoff, Allan. 1992. *The Agrarian Origins of America Capitalism.* Charlottesville: University of Virginia Press.

LaLonde, Robert J. 2007. "The Case for Wage Insurance." Council on Foreign Relations. www.cfr.org/world/case-wage-insurance /p13661.

Lareau, Annette. 2003. *Unequal Childhoods*. Berkeley: University of California Press.

Layard, Richard, Guy Mayraz, and Stephen J. Nickell. 2008. "The Marginal Utility of Income." *Journal of Public Economics* 92: 1846–1857.

Lebergott, Stanley. 1976. *The American Economy*. Princeton, NJ: Princeton University Press.

Leduc, Sylvain, and Daniel Wilson. 2012. "Highway Grants: Roads to Prosperity." *Federal Reserve Bank of San Francisco Economic Letter* 35. www.frbsf.org/economic-research/publications/economic-letter/2012/november/highway-grants/.

Lee, Chul-In, and Gary Solon. 2009. "Trends in Intergenerational Income Mobility." *Review of Economics and Statistics* 91: 766–772.

Lindbeck, Assar, and Dennis J. Snower. 1988. *The Insider-Outsider Theory of Employment and Unemployment*. Cambridge, MA: MIT Press.

———. 2001. "Insiders versus Outsiders." *Journal of Economic Perspectives* 15 (1): 165–188.

Lindert, Peter H. 1994. "The Rise of Social Spending, 1880–1930." *Explorations in Economic History* 31 (1): 1–37.

———. 2004. *Growing Public: Social Spending and Economic Growth since the Eighteenth Century*. 2 vols. Cambridge, UK: Cambridge University Press.

———. 2014. "Private Welfare and the Welfare State." In *The Cambridge History of Capitalism*. Vol. 2: *The Spread of Capitalism*, edited by Larry Neal and Jeffrey. G. Williamson, 464–500. Cambridge, UK: Cambridge University Press.

Lustig, Nora. 2011. "Fiscal Policy and Income Redistribution in Latin America: Challenging the Conventional Wisdom." Tulane University Economics Working Paper 1124, Tulane University. stonecenter.tulane.edu/uploads/Lustig.Fiscal_Policy_and_Income_Redistribution_in_Latin_America.June2011-1344004390.pdf.

Luxembourg Income Study. 2015. Luxembourg Income Study Database. www.lisdatacenter.org.

Lynch, Julia. 2001. "The Age-Orientation of Social Policy Regimes in OECD Countries". *Journal of Social Policy* 30: 411–436.

————. 2006. *Age in the Welfare State.* Cambridge, UK: Cambridge University Press.

MacLeod, Jay. 2009. *Ain't No Makin' It.* 3rd ed. Boulder, CO: Westview.

Maddison, Angus. 2010. "Historical Statistics of the World Economy: 1–2008 AD." Data set. Accessed April 4, 2015, www.ggdc.net /maddison/Historical_Statistics/horizontal-file_02–2010.xls.

Maddison Project. 2013. "The Maddison Project, 2013 Version." www .ggdc.net/maddison/maddison-project/home.htm.

Madrick, Jeff. 2009. *The Case for Big Government.* Princeton, NJ: Princeton University Press.

————. 2011. *Age of Greed: The Triumph of Finance and the Decline of America, 1970 to the Present.* New York: Knopf.

Malkiel, Burton G. 2013. "Asset Management Fees and the Growth of Finance." *Journal of Economic Perspectives* 27 (2): 97–108.

Mankiw, N. Gregory, Matthew Weinzierl, and Danny Yagan. 2009. "Optimal Taxation in Theory and Practice." *Journal of Economic Perspectives* 23 (4): 147–174.

Mayer, Susan E. 1999. *What Money Can't Buy.* Cambridge, MA: Harvard University Press.

McBride, William. 2012. "What Is The Evidence on Taxes and Growth?" Special Report 207. Washington, DC: Tax Foundation. www.taxfoundation.org/article/what-evidence-taxes-and-growth.

McLanahan, Sara. 2001. "Life without Father: What Happens to the Children?" Center for Research on Child Wellbeing, Princeton University.

McLanahan, Sara, and Gary Sandefur. 1994. *Growing Up with a Single Parent.* Cambridge, MA: Harvard University Press.

Meghir, Costas, and David Phillips. 2010. "Labour Supply and Taxes." In *Dimensions of Tax Design: The Mirrlees Review,* edited by James Mirrlees, Stuart Adam, Timothy Besley, Richard Blundell, Stephen Bond, Robert Chote, Malcom Gammie, Paul Johnson, Gareth Myles, and James Poterba, 203–274. Oxford: Oxford University Press.

Mendes, Elizabeth. 2012. "More Than Three in 10 in U.S. Put Off Treatment Due to Cost." *Gallup.com,* December 14.

Mishel, Lawrence, Josh Bivens, Elise Bould, and Heidi Shierholz. 2012. *The State of Working America*. Ithaca: Cornell University Press.

Mishel, Lawrence, and Heidi Shierholz. 2013. "A Lost Decade, Not a Burst Bubble: The Declining Living Standards of Middle-Class Households in the US and Britain." In *The Squeezed Middle: The Pressure on Ordinary Workers in America and Britain*, edited by Sophia Parker, 17–30. Bristol, UK: Policy Press.

Moffitt, Robert, and Mark Wilhelm. 2000. "Taxation and the Labor Supply Decisions of the Affluent." In *Does Atlas Shrug? The Economic Consequences of Taxing the Rich*, edited by Joel Slemrod, 193–234. Cambridge, MA: Harvard University Press.

Morduch, Jonathan, and Rachel Schneider. 2014. "Spikes and Dips: How Income Uncertainty Affects Households." US Financial Diaries. usfinancialdiaries.org/issue1-spikes.

Morgen, Sandra, Joan Acker, and Jill Weigt. 2010. *Stretched Thin: Poor Families, Welfare Work, and Welfare Reform*. Ithaca: Cornell University Press.

Moss, David A. 2002. *When All Else Fails: Government as the Ultimate Risk Manager*. Cambridge, MA: Harvard University Press.

Munnell, Alicia H. 2012. "Bigger and Better: Redesigning Our Retirement System in the Wake of the Financial Collapse." In *Shared Responsibility, Shared Risk*, edited by Jacob S. Hacker and Ann O'Leary, 204–228. Oxford: Oxford University Press.

Murphy, Kevin, Andrei Shleifer, and Robert W. Vishny. 1991. "The Allocation of Talent: Implications for Growth." *Quarterly Journal of Economics* 106: 503–530.

Murray, Charles. 2012. *Coming Apart: The State of White America, 1960–2010*. New York: Crown Forum.

Myles, Gareth. 2000. "Taxation and Economic Growth." *Fiscal Studies* 21 (1): 141–168.

National Center for Education Statistics. 2012. "The Condition of Education." US Department of Education. nces.ed.gov/pubs2012/2012045.pdf.

National Commission on Higher Education Attainment. 2013. "An Open Letter to College and University Leaders: College Completion Must Be Our Priority." American Council on Education.

acenet.edu/news-room/Documents/An-Open-Letter-to-College-and-University-Leaders.pdf.

Okun, Arthur. 1975. *Equality and Efficiency: The Big Tradeoff.* Washington, DC: Brookings Institution Press.

Organization for Economic Cooperation and Development. 1982. "OECD Economic Outlook, Statistics and Projections, No. 31." Accessed March 31, 2015. dx.doi.org/10.1787/data-00135-en.

———. 1992. "OECD Economic Outlook, Statistics and Projections, No. 51." Accessed March 31, 2015. dx.doi.org/10.1787/data-00115-en.

———. 2000. "OECD Economic Outlook, Statistics and Projections, No. 67." Accessed March 31, 2015. dx.doi.org/10.1787/data-00099-en.

———. 2006. "Starting Strong II: Early Childhood Education and Care." www.oecd.org/edu/school/startingstrongiiearlychildhoodeducationandcare.htm.

———. 2008. "Growing Unequal? Income Distribution and Poverty in OECD Countries." www.oecd.org/els/soc/growingunequalincomedistributionandpovertyinoecdcountries.htm

———. 2010. "Education at a Glance 2010." www.oecd.org/edu/skills-beyond-school/educationataglance2010oecdindicators.htm.

———. 2012. "Education at a Glance 2012." www.oecd-ilibrary.org/education/education-at-a-glance-2012_eag-2012-en.

———. 2015a. "Dataset: Table I.7: Top Statutory Personal Income Tax Rate and Top Marginal Tax Rates for Employees." Accessed August 10, 2015. stats.oecd.org/Index.aspx?DataSetCode=TABLE_I7.

———. 2015b. "In It Together: Why Less Inequality Benefits All." Accessed May 29, 2015. dx.doi.org/10.1787/9789264235120-en.

———. 2015c. "OECD Economic Outlook, Statistics and Projections, No. 97." Accessed August 18, 2015. dx.doi.org/10.1787/data-00759-en.

———. 2015d. "OECD Employment Outlook." Accessed January 7, 2015. www.oecd.org/els/oecd-employment-outlook-19991266.htm.

———. 2015e. "OECD National Accounts at a Glance." Database. Accessed August 19, 2015. dx.doi.org/10.1787/data-00369-en.

———. 2015f. "OECD Tax Statistics." Database. Accessed August 18, 2015. dx.doi.org/10.1787/tax-data-en.

Ostry, Jonathan D., Andrew Berg, and Charalambos G. Tsangarides. 2014. "Redistribution, Inequality, and Growth." February 17. IMF Staff Discussion Note SDN/14/02X. www.imf.org/external/pubs /ft/sdn/2014/sdn1402.pdf.

Parlapiano, Alicia. 2012. "Unmarried Households Are Increasingly the Norm." *New York Times,* July 14.

Pessoa, João Paolo, and John Van Reenen. 2012. "Decoupling of Wage Growth and Productivity Growth: Myth and Reality." Commission on Living Standards, Resolution Foundation. resolutionfoundation.org/publications/decoupling-wage-growth-productivity -growth-myth-reality.

Pestieau, Pierre. 2006. *The Welfare State in the European Union: Economic and Social Perspectives.* Oxford: Oxford University Press.

Pew Research Center. 2012. "Trends in American Values: 1987–2012." people-press.org/files/legacy-pdf/06–04–12%20Values%20 Release.pdf.

Phillips, Meredith. 2011. "Parenting, Time Use, and Disparities in Academic Outcomes." In *Whither Opportunity? Rising Inequality, Schools, and Children's Life Chances,* edited by Greg J. Duncan and Richard J. Murnane, 207–228. New York: Russell Sage Foundation.

Piketty, Thomas, and Emmanuel Saez. 2003. "Income Inequality in the United States, 1913–1998." *Quarterly Journal of Economics* 118 (1): 1–39. Tables and figures updated through 2014 at http://eml.berkeley .edu//~saez/TabFig2014prel.xls.

Piketty, Thomas, Emmanuel Saez, and Stefanie Stantcheva. 2014. "Optimal Taxation of Top Incomes: A Tale of Three Elasticities." *American Economic Journal: Economic Policy* 6: 230–271.

Pofeldt, Elaine. 2014. "Obama: Is the Job of the Future a Freelance One?" *CNBC,* January 29.

Prescott, Edward C. 2004a. "Why Do Americans Work So Much More than Europeans?" *Federal Reserve Bank of Minneapolis Quarterly Review* 28: 2–13.

———. 2004b. "Why Do Americans Work More Than Europeans?" *Wall Street Journal.* October 21.

Prichard, Wilson, Alex Cobham, and Andrew Goodall. 2014. "The ICTD Government Revenue Dataset." September. International

Centre for Tax and Development Working Paper No. 19. Institute for Development Studies, Brighton, UK. Accessed January 14, 2015. www.ictd.ac/images/ICTD%20WP19_2.pdf.

Pritchett, Lant, and Eric Werker. 2012. "Developing the Guts of a GUT (Grand Unified Theory): Elite Commitment and Inclusive Growth." December 7. ESID Working Paper Series 16/12, Accessed April 24, 2015. r4d.dfid.gov.uk/PDF/Outputs/ESID/esid_wp_16_pritchett_werker.pdf.

Psacharapoulos George, and Harry Anthony Patrinos. 2004a. "Returns to Investment in Education: A Further Update." *Education Economics* 12: 2 (August): 111–134.

———. 2004b. "Human Capital and Rates of Return." In *International Handbook on the Economics of Education*, edited by Geraint Johnes and Jill Johnes, 1–57. Cheltenham, UK: Edward Elgar.

Putnam, Robert. 2015. *Our Kids*. New York: Simon and Schuster.

Rank, Mark Robert, Thomas A. Hirschl, and Kirk A. Foster. 2013. *Chasing the American Dream*. New York: Oxford University Press.

Rawls, John. 1971. *A Theory of Justice*. Cambridge, MA: Harvard University Press.

Reardon, Sean. 2011. "The Widening Academic-Achievement Gap Between the Rich and the Poor: New Evidence and Possible Explanations." In *Whither Opportunity? Rising Inequality, Schools, and Children's Life Chances*, edited by Greg J. Duncan and Richard J. Murnane, 91–115. New York: Russell Sage.

Rector, Robert. 2007. "How Poor Are America's Poor?" Backgrounder 2064, Heritage Foundation. heritage.org/research/reports/2007/08/how-poor-are-americas-poor-examining-the-plague-of-poverty-in-america.

Reid, T. R. 2009. *The Healing of America*. New York: Penguin.

Reinhardt, Uwe E. 2000. "Health Care for the Aging Baby Boom: Lessons from Abroad." *Journal of Economic Perspectives* 14 (2): 71–84.

Robinson, Leslie, and Joel Slemrod. 2012. "Understanding Multidimensional Tax Systems." *International Tax and Public Finance* 19: 237–267.

Rodrik, Dani. 2007. *One Economics, Many Recipes: Globalization, Institutions, and Economic Growth*. Princeton, NJ: Princeton University Press.

Roemer, John E. 1998. *Equality of Opportunity.* Cambridge, MA: Harvard University Press.

Rogerson, Richard, 2007. "Taxation and Market Work: Is Scandinavia an Outlier?" *Economic Theory* 32: 59–85.

Roin, Benjamin N. 2009. "Unpatentable Drugs and the Standards of Patentability." *Texas Law Review* 87: 503–570.

Romer, Paul M. 1986. "Increasing Returns and Long-run Growth." *Journal of Political Economy* 94: 1002–1037.

———. 1987. "Growth Based on Increasing Returns to Specialization." *Journal of Political Economy* 94: 1002–1037.

———. 1990. "Endogenous Technical Change." *Journal of Political Economy* 98: 71–102.

Rose, Stephen J., and Scott Winship. 2009. "Ups and Downs: Does the American Economy Still Promote Upward Mobility?" Economic Mobility Project. pewtrusts.org/en/research-and-analysis/reports /2009/06/18/ups-and-downs-does-the-american-economy-still-promote-upward-mobility.

Rosen, Harvey, and Ted Gayer. 2009. *Public Finance.* 9th ed. New York: McGraw-Hill/Irwin.

Ruffing, Kathy A. 2011. "What the 2011 Trustees' Report Shows about Social Security." Center on Budget and Policy Priorities. cbpp .org/research/what-the-2011-trustees-report-shows-about-social -security.

Ruhm, Christopher, and Jane Waldfogel. 2011. "Long-Term Effects of Early Childcare and Education." Discussion Paper 6149, Institute for the Study of Labor. ftp.iza.org/dp6149.pdf.

Saez, Emmanuel. 2004. "Reported Incomes and Marginal Tax Rates, 1960–2000: Evidence and Policy Implications." In *Tax Policy and the Economy*, vol. 18, edited by James M. Poterba, 117–174. Cambridge, MA: MIT Press.

Saez, Emmanuel, Joel Slemrod, and Seth Giertz. 2012. "The Elasticity of Taxable Income with Respect to Marginal Tax Rates: A Critical Review." *Journal of Economic Literature* 50 (1): 3–50.

Saez, Emmanuel, and Stefanie Stantcheva. 2016. "Generalized Social Marginal Welfare Weights for Optimal Tax Theory." *American Economic Review* 106: 24–45.

Sampson, Robert. 2012. *Great American City.* Chicago: University of Chicago Press.

Schwartz, Christine R., and Robert D. Mare. 2005. "Trends in Educational Assortative Marriage from 1940 to 2003." *Demography* 42: 621–646.

Scruggs, Lyle, and James Allan. 2005. "The Material Consequences of Welfare States: Benefit Generosity and Absolute Poverty in 16 OECD Countries." April. Luxembourg Income Study Working Paper 409. lisdatacenter.org/wps/liswps/409.pdf.

Sellers, Charles. 1994. *The Market Revolution: Jacksonian Democracy, 1815–1846.* Oxford: Oxford University Press.

Shaefer, H. Luke, and Marci Ybarra. 2012. "The Welfare Reforms of the 1990s and the Stratification of Material Well-Being among Low-Income Households with Children." *Children and Youth Services Review* 34: 1810–1817.

Sharkey, Patrick. 2013. *Stuck in Place: Urban Neighborhoods and the End of Progress Toward Racial Equality.* Chicago: University of Chicago Press.

Shiller, Robert J. 2003. *The New Financial Order.* Princeton, NJ: Princeton University Press.

Shlaes, Amity. 2008. *The Forgotten Man: A New History of the Great Depression.* New York: Harper.

Slemrod, Joel. 1995. "What Do Cross-Country Studies Teach Us about Government Involvement, Prosperity, and Economic Growth?" *Brookings Papers on Economic Activity* 2: 373–415.

———. 2006. "The Consequences of Taxation." In *Taxation, Economic Prosperity, and Distributive Justice,* edited by Ellen Frankel Paul, Fred D. Miller Jr., Jeffrey Paul, 73–87. Cambridge, UK: Cambridge University Press.

Slemrod, Joel, and Jon Bakija. 2016. *Taxing Ourselves: A Citizen's Guide to the Debate over Taxes.* 5th ed. Cambridge, MA: MIT Press.

Smeeding, Timothy M., Lee Rainwater, and Gary Burtless. 2000. "United States Poverty in a Cross-National Context". September. Luxembourg Income Study Working Paper 244. lisdatacenter.org /wps/liswps/244.pdf.

Smith, Adam. (1766) 1978. *Lectures on Jurisprudence.* Edited by R.L. Meek, D.D. Raphael, and P.G. Stein. Oxford: Clarendon Press.

————. (1776) 1993. *An Inquiry into the Nature and Causes of the Wealth of Nations.* Edited by Kathryn Sutherland. New York: Oxford University Press.

Solow, Robert M. 1957. "Technical Change and the Aggregate Production Function." *Review of Economics and Statistics* 39: 312–320.

Soltas, Evan. 2013. "The Myth of the Falling Bridge." *Bloomberg View,* April 8.

Stiglitz, Joseph E. 2009. "Regulation and Failure." In *New Perspectives on Regulation,* edited by David Moss and John Cisternino, 11–23. Cambridge, MA: Tobin Project.

Stiglitz, Joseph E., and Jay Rosengard. 2015. *Economics of the Public Sector.* 4th ed. New York: W.W. Norton.

Stiglitz, Joseph E., and Andrew Weiss. 1981. "Credit Rationing in Markets with Imperfect Information." *American Economic Review* 71: 393–419.

Stokey, Nancy L., and Sergio Rebelo. 1995. "Growth Effects of Flat-Rate Taxes." *Journal of Political Economy* 103: 519–550.

Stuart, Alix. 2011. "Missing: Public Companies: Why Is the Number of Publicly Traded Companies in the U.S. Declining?" *CFO.com,* March 22. Accessed May 25, 2012. www.cfo.com/article.cfm/14563859.

Swan, T.W. 1956. "Economic Growth and Capital Accumulation." *Economic Record* 32: 334–361.

Tanzi, Vito. 2011. *Governments versus Markets: The Changing Economic Role of the State.* Cambridge, UK: Cambridge University Press.

Tanzi, Vito, and Ludger Schuknecht. 2000. *Public Spending in the 20th Century. A Global Perspective.* Cambridge, UK: Cambridge University Press.

Thomasson, Melissa A. 2002. "From Sickness to Health: The Twentieth Century Development of U.S. Health Insurance." *Explorations in Economic History* 39: 233–253.

————. 2003. "The Importance of Group Coverage: How Tax Policy Shaped U.S. Health Insurance." *American Economic Review* 93: 1373–1384.

Urban-Brookings Tax Policy Center. 2013a. "Table T13–0180: Share of Federal Taxes; All Tax Units by Expanded Cash Income Percentile, 2014, Baseline; Current Law." July 25. Accessed March 24, 2015. www.taxpolicycenter.org/numbers/Content/Excel/T13-0180.xls.

———. 2013b. "Table T13-0185: Effective Marginal Tax Rates on Wages, Salaries, and Capital Income by Expanded Cash Income Percentile, 2012." July 25. Accessed March 24, 2015. www.taxpolicy center.org/numbers/Content/Excel/T13-0186.xls.

———. 2013c. "Table T13-0186: Effective Marginal Tax Rates on Wages, Salaries, and Capital Income by Expanded Cash Income Percentile, 2013." July 25. Accessed March 24, 2015. www.taxpolicy center.org/numbers/Content/Excel/T13-0185.xls.

US Bureau of Economic Analysis. 2015. "National Income and Product Accounts of the United States." Accessed April 4, 2015. www.bea .gov/national/.

US House Committee on Ways and Means. 2014. *Green Book*. green-book.waysandmeans.house.gov.

US Senate Committee on Health, Education, Labor, and Pensions. 2012. "The Retirement Crisis and a Plan to Solve It." July. ameri-canbenefitscouncil.org/pub/e6139ba3-a4f9-ab37-7a1d-f11a89dd2c37.

Vandell, Deborah Lowe, and Barbara Wolfe. 2000. "Child Care Quality: Does It Matter and Does It Need to Be Improved?" Special Report 78. Institute for Research on Poverty, University of Wisconsin-Madison. irp.wisc.edu/publications/sr/pdfs/sr78 .pdf.

Wagner, Adolph. (1883) 1958. "The Nature of the Fiscal Economy." Translated by Nancy Cooke. In *Classics in the Theory of Public Finance*, edited by Richard A. Musgrave and Alan T. Peacock, 1–8. New York: Macmillan.

Waldfogel, Jane. 2006. *What Children Need*. Cambridge, MA: Harvard University Press.

———. 2009. "The Role of Family Policies in Antipoverty Policy." *Focus* 26 (2): 50–55.

Wang, Chen, Koen Caminada, and Kees Goudswaard. 2012. "The Redistributive Effect of Social Transfer Programmes and Taxes: A Decomposition across Countries." *International Social Security Review* 65 (3): 27–48.

Weber, Caroline E. 2014. "Toward Obtaining a Consistent Estimate of the Elasticity of Taxable Income Using Difference-in-Differences." *Journal of Public Economics* 117: 90–103.

Weeden, Kim A. 2002. "Why Do Some Occupations Pay More Than Others? Social Closure and Earnings Inequality in the United States." *American Journal of Sociology* 108: 55–101.

Western, Bruce. 2006. *Punishment and Inequality in America*. New York: Russell Sage Foundation.

Western, Bruce, and Jake Rosenfeld. 2011. "Unions, Norms, and the Rise in U.S. Wage Inequality." *American Sociological Review* 76: 513–537.

Wilson, William Julius. 1978. *The Declining Significance of Race*. Chicago: University of Chicago Press.

———. 1987. *The Truly Disadvantaged*. Chicago: University of Chicago Press.

———. 1996. *When Work Disappears*. New York: Vintage.

———. 2009. *More Than Just Race*. New York: W. W. Norton.

Winship, Scott. 2012. "Bogeyman Economics." *National Affairs*, Winter: 3–21.

Wolff, Edward N. 2011. *The Transformation of the American Pension System*. Kalamazoo, MI: Upjohn Institute.

Woodlander, Steffie, Terry Campbell, and David U. Himmelstein. 2003. "Costs of Health Care Administration in the United States and Canada." *New England Journal of Medicine* 349: 768–775.

World Bank. 2015. "World Development Indicators." Accessed July 28, 2015. data.worldbank.org/data-catalog/world-development-indicators.

World Economic Forum. 2012. "The Global Competitiveness Report 2012–2013." weforum.org/reports/global-competitiveness-report-2012–2013.

———. 2015. "The Global Competitiveness Report 2013–2014." weforum.org/reports/global-competitiveness-report-2014–2015.

Wright, Erik Olin, and Rachel Dwyer. 2003. "The Patterns of Job Expansions in the United States: A Comparison of the 1960s and 1990s." *Socio-Economic Review* 1: 289–325.

Yglesias, Matthew. 2012. *The Rent Is Too Damn High.* New York: Simon and Schuster.

Zandi, Mark. 2011. "An Analysis of the Obama Jobs Plan." *Moody's Analytics: Dismal Scientist,* September 9.

Zingales, Luigi. 2012. *A Capitalism for the People.* New York: Basic Books.

———. 2015. "Does Finance Benefit Society?" NBER Working Paper 20894, National Bureau of Economic Research. www.nber.org /papers/w20894.

INDEX

Adams, John Quincy, 6
adverse selection, 73, 74
Affordable Care Act (2010), 51, 136,
    156n7
Agell, Jonas, 157n18
aging population, viii, 28, 37, 65. *See
    also* elderly
Aid to Families with Dependent
    Children (AFDC), 14, 138
Alesina, Alberto, 111, 114, 117–18,
    163n51
American Recovery and Reinvest-
    ment Act (2009), 13
American Society of Civil
    Engineers, 12
Angrist, Joshua D., 160n32
Antitrust laws, 8
Army, US, 8
Athens, 2004 Summer Olympics
    in, 55
Australia, 58
Austria, 36

Bakija, Jon, 136

bankruptcy protection, 13
Belgium, 36, 94
Bergh, Andreas, 102–3, 107, 108,
    157n18, 163n49
Bleaney, Michael, 150n7, 153n20
Blomquist, Soren, 118
boom and bust cycles, 9
Botswana, 157n17
Britain, *see* United Kingdom
budgets, 56, 58–59, 64, 65;
    balancing, vii, 10, 153n31; deficits,
    vii, ix, 10, 37, 45, 100; of welfare
    states, 36, 37, 44, 47, 54, 152n9
business cycles, ix, 9, 100–104, 112

Calhoun, John, 6
California, 12, 41; University of,
    Berkeley, 7
Canada, 24, 58, 86, 159n29; health
    care in, 46, 49
canals, 5–6
Capitalism and Freedom (Friedman),
    150n2
carbon tax, 30

Carneiro, Pedro, 60
Census Bureau, US, Current
Population Survey, 146n16
Center on Budget and Policy
Priorities, 155 56n7
Chetty, Raj, 109, 118, 120
Chicago, University of, 11
childcare, 21, 23, 28, 120
child labor, 8
Children's Health Insurance
Program (CHIP), 156n7
Child Tax Credit, 24, 29, 138
China, 157n17
Civil Rights Act (1964), 11
Civil War, 7
Clay, Henry, 6
Cole, Adam, 130
college. *See* higher education
Commanding the Heights (Yergin),
145n3
commercialization, 5
communications technology, 126
Congress, US, 11
Connecticut, 41
Constant, Amelie F., 163n51
Constitution, US, 4
consumer markets, transformation
of, 9
consumption taxes, 30, 47, 105,
155n2
Corn Laws, 35
corruption, 7; low levels of, 37, 45,
152n12
counterfactuals, social-budget,
58–60
Crash of 1819, 9
Crash of 1929, 10
cross-country comparison on
taxes and government spending
as percentage of GDP, 68, 75–121,
162n45; common ground on,
106–8; econometric evidence on,

95–106, *96–98;* at given time,
76–79, *78;* labor supply and,
109–21, *113;* relative changes over
time of, 79–83; since early 1960s,
93–95, 164n59; very long run,
83–93, *84, 85, 90*
Cutler, David, 168n92
Cyprus, 54

Dalgaard, Carl-Johan, 107
Davis, Steven J., 164n59
deadweight loss, 70–71, 118–24, 128,
133–34, 154–55n1, 163n54, 165n65,
166n70, 168n85, 169n94
Defense Department, US, 9
deficits, vii, ix, 10, 37, 45, 100
Denmark, 22, 24, 36, 94, 115, 140. *See
also* Nordic countries
deposit insurance, 10
Diamond, Peter, 169n97
Dickey-Fuller test, 159n25
disaster relief, 14
distributive justice, 72–75
drinking water, clean, 8–9, 13

early education, 22–23, 28, 29, 138
Earned Income Tax Credit
(EITC), 2, 14, 26, 120, 138,
149n80; for childless households,
16; indexing, 28–29, 149n79
East Asia, 61, 82. *See also specific
nations*
Easterly, William, 160n31
Economic Freedom Index, 103, 108
economic security, x, 2, 12–19, 67,
135–38
economies of scale, 7, 47
Eisenhower, Dwight D., 11
elderly, 2, 38, 56–62, *59,* 65, 67. *See
also* Medicare; Social Security
elementary school. *See* public
education

employee protection laws (EPLs), 55
employment, 2, 14–17, 25–28, 30, 137;
  correlations of taxes and, 115, 121;
  effects of social spending on, 38,
  43, 139; equality of opportunity
  for, 19, 20; inflexibility of terms
  of, 110, investment in infrastructure and, 13; manufacturing, 22,
  25; of women, 23. *See also*
  unemployment
energy assistance, 17, 138
England, 35. *See also* United
  Kingdom
Enns, Peter K., 162n44
entrepreneurship, 75, 123
Equatorial Guinea, 157n17
Erie Canal, 6

Faggio, Giulia, 164n60
Family and Medical Leave Act
  (1993), 18
family structure, changes in, 20
Federal Highway Administration,
  12
Federalist Papers, The, 5
Federal Reserve, 9, 27
Feenstra, Robert C., 161n35
female/male wage ratios, 52–53, 53
finance industry, 130–32; inadequate regulation of, 9–10, 37
financial derivatives, systemic
  risks of, 54
financial transactions tax, 30
Finland, 24, 36, 94, 151n7. *See also*
  Nordic Countries
Folster, Stefan, 157n18
food stamps, 11, 26, 138
Ford, Henry, 9
Foster, Kirk, 146n22
401(k)s, 17
France, 6, 58, 94, 114; decline
  in hours worked in, 114;

employment rate in, 121; public
  education in, 6, 36
Fraser Institute Economic
  Freedom Index, 108
free enterprise, 9
free lunch, 36–45, 106–7, 140
free trade, 108
Friedman, Milton, 150n2
Furman, Jason, 155n5

Garfinkel, Irwin, 150n4
Gemmell, Norman, 104–7, 151n7,
  153n20, 162n44
Germany, 36, 54, 114, 151n7
GI Bill, 11, 138
Giertz, Seth, 167n77
Glaeser, Edward, 111, 114, 117–18,
  163n51
globalization, 22, 126, 133, 141
Gordon, Roger, 150n3
Great Depression, 10, 64, 158n22
Great Recession, 54, 114
Greece, 55, 94–95, 98, 113, 122,
  161nn35, 161–62n36
Greenspan Commission on Social
  Security Reform, 63
gross domestic product (GDP), 2,
  12, 13, 20, 74–75, 120, 132, 153n32,
  156n9; annual pension payouts
  indexed to, 64; causal effects of
  taxes on, 79–80; finance as share
  of, 131; government expenditures
  as percentage of, 31, 36–37, 50, 52,
  59, 68, 136, 139, 141, 150n4, 152n9,
  157–58n20, 160n32; net effects of
  social programs on, 40, 42–54,
  40, 56, 58, 60; per capita, 2, 25,
  28–41, 39, 40, 147n17, 157n19,
  158nn22,23, 159n25, 160–61nn33,
  35, 161nn36,45, 167n83; per hour
  worked, *see* productivity; rate of
  real growth in, 70; tax revenue

gross domestic product *(continued)*
as percentage of, *48, 122,* 158n13,
161n36, 162n45, 164n57; world,
160n34. *See also* cross-country
comparison on taxes and
government spending as
percentage of GDP
Growing Public (Lindert), 106
Guinea, Equatorial, 157n17

Hamilton, Alexander, 4–5
Harrington, Michael, 11
Hausmann, Ricardo, 157n19
Head Start, 138
health insurance and care, 15, 28,
37, 51–52, 67, 74, 150n4, 151n4;
efficient, 48–49; life expectancy
and, 45, 50; preventive, 59;
universal, 19, 29, 46, 49, 138. *See
also* Medicaid; Medicare
Heckman, James, 60, 155n5
Heim, Brad, 130
Henrekson, Magnus, 157n18,
163n49, 164n59
higher education, 11, 20, 22–24, 129,
138, 168*n*
high school. *See* public education
Hirschl, Thomas, 146n22
homeownership, 13
Hong Kong, 82, 157n17
hours worked, correlation of taxes
with, 74–75, 110–14, 116–21,
164–66n65
household incomes, 13–17, 26,
28–29, 146n16, 152n9. *See also*
low-income households
housing assistance, 17, 138
human capital, women's, 52–53,
141

Iceland, 54, 161n35
immigrants, 25, 38, 56

incentives, 33, 42, 79, 99, 107, 109,
155n2, 168n87; labor supply, 111,
115, 118–20, 154n1, 164n59; of social
spending, 42, 139, 140; tax, 47, 67,
69, 76, 121–23, 126–28, 130, 133
income inequality, x, 2, 19–21,
166n71, 168nn88,90; due to
unfairly shared prosperity, 13,
24–29
income tax, 47, 105, 124, 133, 154n1;
marginal rates of, 70, 76, 123–24,
125, 127–28, *129,* 133, 167n78, 168n88,
169n96; top rates of, 30, 69–70,
119, *125,* 130, 166n71, 169nn94,97
indentured servants, 4
industrialization, 7–8, 68, 81, 82, 141;
cross-country comparisons of
GDP and, 83–94, 158nn22,23,
159n26
industrial policy, 4–5, 82, 145n3
infant mortality, 49
inflation, 17, 27, 62, 75, 103, 161n35;
minimum wage indexed to, 16,
25
infrastructure, x, 5–7, 11–13, 33, 34,
138; economic benefits of
investing in, 28, 105, 107, 139, 143;
need for government spending
on, viii, 2, 12–13, 29, 68, 136
Inklaar, Robert, 161n35
innovation, 9, 71, 75, 91, 139, 140,
156n8
interest rates, 13, 100, 161n36
Internal Revenue Service (IRS),
US, 47, *48,* 130, 166n71, 169n96
Internet, 8–9, 12
Ireland, 37, *54,* 58, 158n20,
159nn25,29
Italy, 36, 61, 94

Jackson, Andrew, 9
Jacobs, Elizabeth, 146n22

Jäntti, Markus, 116–18, 165–66n65
Japan, 39, 49, 52; budget deficit of, 37
Jefferson, Thomas, 1–5, 150n2
Jones, Charles I., 87, 107, 158n22, 159n25

Karlsson, Martin, 102–3, 107, 108, 157n18
Karras, Georgios, 106
Kelly, Nathan J., 162n44
Keynes, John Maynard, 10
King, Gary, 162n39
Kleven, Henrik, 114–15, 156–57n13, 165n63
Kneller, Richard, 104–7, 151n7, 153n20, 162n44
Knuse, Agneta, 153n32
Kreiner, Claus Thustrup, 107
Krugman, Paul, 161n36
K и education, 6, 29, 138

labor markets, 16, 25, 27–28, 121, 150; opportunity gap for success in, 23; protection of vested interests in, 37, 141
laissez-faire, 3, 10, 135
land ownership, 4
Lectures on Jurisprudence (Smith), 34
Li, Wei, 156n13
life-expectancy, 45, 49, 50, 52, 61–64, 140, 152n9
limited liability law, 13
Lincoln, Abraham, 7
Lindert, Peter, 104, 106, 121, 136, 153n31
London, nineteenth-century, 8
longevity. *See* life-expectancy
Louisiana Purchase, 4
low-income households, x, 2, 14, 19–24, 137; earnings of, 26, 28,

149n80; of elderly, 17. *See also* income inequality
Lucas, Robert, 11
Luxembourg, 94–95, 98, 113, 122, 159n25, 161n35; Income Study, 116, 148n16, 152n11
Lynch, Julia, 58

Maddison Project, 157–58n20, 160n34
Madison, James, 5
Madrick, Jeff, 136
market crashes, 9, 10, 26, 54
market failures, 72–74, 134, 155nn5,6
marketing, mass, 9
Maryland, 6
Masaki, Takaaki, 162n44
Massachusetts, 6
Massachusetts Institute of Technology, 1
mass marketing, 9
mass production, 9
Medicaid, 2, 11, 14, 51, 156n7
Medicare, 2, 11, 14, 19, 51, 58, 139, 156n7
Mediterranean Europe, 37, 54, 55. *See also specific nations*
Meghir, Costas, 119–20
middle class, 10, 13, 25–26, 28, 56, 66; opportunity to rise to, 2, 20, 22, 135, 137
minimum wage, 14–16, 25, 27–29, 138, 149n80
Moffitt, Robert, 119
Morgan, J. P., 9
Morrill Act (1853), 7
mothers, human capital of, 52–53
Murphy, Kevin, 168n93

national bank, US, 4
Netherlands, 36, 94
"new classicals," 11

New Deal, 1, 10
New York City, 9
New York State, 5–6
New Zealand, 158n20
Nickell, Stephen, 164n60
Nordic countries, 68, 101, 142;
    challenges of aging population
    in, 65; economic security
    ensured in, 15; efficiency of
    public policies in, 107–8;
    equalization of opportunity in,
    22–23; female-male wage ratios
    in, 52–53; innovation in, 156n8;
    prosperity in, 54. See also
    Denmark; Finland; Norway;
    Sweden
Norway, 24, 36, 94, 115, 140. See also
Nordic countries

Ohio State University, 7
Ohlsson, Henry, 157n18
Okun, Arthur, 71, 119
Olympic Games, 55
opportunity deficit, 2, 19–22, 134, 137;
    government programs to reduce,
    x, 12, 13, 22–24, 67, 72, 75, 138
Organization for Economic
    Co-operation and Development
    (OECD) countries, 104–6, 116,
    150n4, 155n5, 157–58n20, 167n83;
    aging of adult populations in,
    57, 65; growth and prosperity in,
    40; life expectancy in, 45;
    Luxembourg Income Study, 116,
    148n16, 152n11; work-life balance
    for parents in, 52
Other America, The (Harrington), 11
Otterbach, Steffen, 163n51

paid parental leave, 2, 18, 19, 52, 138
Panel Study of Income Dynamics
    (PSID), 146n22, 147n44

Panic of 1917, 9
parental leave, 2, 18, 19, 52, 138
payroll tax, ix, 30, 156n10
Pennsylvania, 6
Penn World Tables Version 8.0,
    157n17, 160n35, 167n83
pensions, 17, 29, 56, 69, 111, 150–51n4,
    153–54n32; impact of recessions
    on, 55; longevity and, 61–65;
    private versus public, 59–60;
    quasi-public, saving require-
    ments for, 82
Pew Research Center, 137
pharmaceutical companies, 31–32
Phillips, David, 119–20
Piketty, Thomas, 128, 130, 133,
    167n84, 168nn85,87,90
Pirttilä, Jukka, 116–18, 165–66n65
Pischke, Jörn-Steffen, 160n32
Portugal, 36, 54, 94–95, 161n35
poverty, 13, 38, 65, 140, 146n22,
    152n11; age and, x, 56–57, 57,
    63; programs to alleviate, 11, 37,
    45, 46 (see also specific programs)
Prescott, Edward, 110–11, 114, 163n54
pre-tax income, 121–29, 167n78
primary school. See public
    education
Pritchett, Lant, 157n19, 158n23
productivity, 110, 121–22, 126, 141
    investment in, 10, 52, 55, 65
progressive taxes, ix, 66, 69–70, 76,
    120, 126, 134
property taxes, 6
prosperity, ix, 3, 10–12, 75–76, 81, 134;
    correlation of social spending
    and, 40, 42; shared, 12, 13, 24–29,
    67, 108, 138; Smith on, 38–39
Prussia, 6
public education, 11, 21–24, 33,
    35–36, 150n2; K-12, 6, 29, 138
publicly traded firms, 131, 168

racial discrimination, 7, 11
railroads, 7, 12
Rainwater, Lee, 150n4
Rank, Mark, 146n22
Rebelo, Sergio, 158n22
recessions, 10, 64, 68, 95, 100–102, 104, 158n23; cycles of booms and, 9, 100; ongoing, in European countries, 95, 161–62n36; of 2001, 26; of 2008–09, vii, 16, 54–55, 114
regulations, government, x, 4–5, 10, 18, 25, 32
rent-seeking activity, 69, 126, 130–32, 168n93
Republicans, Jeffersonian, 5
retirement benefits, 67. *See also* pensions; Social Security
risk-taking, 33, 123, 140
roads, 5, 6, 12, 13, 28
Robinson, Leslie, 156–57n13
Rodrik, Dani,157n19
Rogerson, Richard, 165n63
Roosevelt, Franklin D., 10

Sacerdote, Bruce, 111, 114, 117–18, 163n51
Saez, Emmanuel, 128, 130, 133, 167n77, 167n84, 168nn85,87,90, 169nn94,97
sales taxes, ix, 47
sanitation, 8–9
Sanz, Ismael, 104–7, 151n7, 153n20, 162n44
Schiller, Robert, 149n78
secondary school, *See* public education
Securities and Exchange Commission, 10
Selin, Håkan, 116–18, 165–66n65
Shleifer, Andrei, 168n93
Simula, Laurent, 118

sin taxes, 47
Singapore, 81, 82, 103, 157n17
Slemrod, Joel, 76, 156–57n13, 167n77, 169n94
Smeeding, Timothy M., 150n4
Smith, Adam, 34–36, 38–39, 150n2
SNAP, *see* food stamps
social-budget counterfactuals, 58–60
Social Darwinism, 8, 65
Social Security, 14, 17, 58, 60, 138, 155n7; creation of, 10, 136; disability benefits, 14; expansion of, 11; impact of increased life expectancy on, 61–64; increases in benefit levels of, 26; payroll taxes, 156n10
socioeconomic status, 13–14, 20, 22, 135. *See also* income inequality
Solow, Robert M., 168n31
South Korea, 81, 82, 157n17
Soviet Union, 151n7
Spain, 36, 54, 95
Stantcheva, Stefanie, 128, 130, 133, 167n84, 168nn85,87
State Children's Health Insurance Program, 51
Stiglitz, Joseph E., 155n5
Stokey, Nancy L., 158n22
Summers, Lawrence, 145n3
Supplemental Security Income (SSI), 14
Supreme Court, US, 51
Swan, T. W., 160n31
Sweden, 18, 39, 58, 114, 140; free public higher education in, 24; paid parental leave in, 22; pension reform in, 63–65, 153–54n32; social transfer share of GDP in, 36; subsidies complementary to labor supply in, 115; taxes as percentage of

Sweden *(continued)*
  GDP in, 94. *See also* Nordic
    countries
Switzerland, 86

Taiwan, 82, 103
tariffs, 4, 35
taxes, 1, 11, 24–26, 29, 30, 33, 68, 138;
  on addictive goods, 37; consumption, 30, 47, 105, 155n2; correlation
  of hours worked with, 74–75,
  110–14, 116–21, 164–66n65; costs
  and benefits of, 70–75; efficient
  mix of transfer and, 46–48;
  exemption of employee health
  plans from, 51; payroll, ix, 30,
  156n10; pre-tax income and cuts
  in, 121–33; property, 6, 65; sales,
  ix; Smith's views on, 34–36; social
  spending funded by, 41, 44–45,
  56, 59–60, 67 (*see also* welfare
  states; *types of social programs*).
  See also cross-country comparison on taxes and government
  spending as percentage of GDP;
  Earned Income Tax Credit;
  income tax
Tax Reform Act (1986), 119
technology, x, 9, 10, 70–71, 75, 126,
  132, 141; economic growth and,
  80, 86, 88, 91, 100, 102, 160n31;
  employment impacted by, 22, 25
Temporary Assistance for Needy
  Families (TANF), 14, 16–17, 26,
  138
Texas A&M University, 7
Thailand, 157n17
Thoursie, Peter Skogman, 157n18
Timmer, Marcel P., 161n35
trade, nineteenth century, 5–6, 9
Transparency International,
  152n9

Turkey, 94–95, *98, 113, 122,* 159n25,
  161n35

unemployment, 8, 27, 55, 103–4,
  146n22; GDP per capita and, 95,
  98, 100, 161n36
unemployment insurance, 2, 14, 19,
  26, 43, 45, 138, 150n4, 156n7;
  eligibility criteria for, 18, 29;
  New Deal introduction of, 10;
  during recessions, 101
unions, 10, 27, 119, 164n60; decline
  of, in United States, 2, 22, 25;
  reduction in work hours
  advocated by, 111, 114, 118
United Kingdom, 36, 39; administrative costs of tax collection in,
  47, *48;* health care costs in,
  49–50; labor force participation
  in, 119–21
United States, 1–33, 52, 67–69, 73,
  83, 93, 108, 135–43, 170; administrative costs of tax collection in,
  47, *48;* aging population of,
  61–63, 65; budget deficit of, vii,
  ix, 37; Census Bureau Current
  Population Survey, 146n16;
  cross-country comparisons
  with, 86, 90, 96, 97; differences
  among states in, 41; early
  childhood and primary
  education in, 6, 22–23, 56;
  economic security issues in,
  13–19; employment in, 22, 25–26;
  financial market crash in, 54;
  GDP per capita in, 76, 86, 94,
  158n22, 160n35; health care in, 15,
  18, 49–52; higher education in,
  23–24; incarceration in, 22;
  income inequality in, 2, 19–21,
  26–27, 123, *125,* 166n71, 168nn88,
  90; infrastructure of, 2, 12–13;

innovation in, 156n8; institutional mistakes of, 27; international impact of 2008 recession in, 54; labor force participation in, 121; life expectancy in, 48–49; myth of laissez-faire in, 3–12, 135; national bank of, 4, 9; post-World War II economic growth of, 26, 86; poverty by age in, x, 24, 57–58, 146; recommendations for public programs in, 29–30; Southern states of, 41; success of New Deal in, 10; taxes in, 47, 67, 94, 118–19, 121, 123, 128–30, 133–34, 151n4, 158n22, 164n58, 169n97; work hours in, 8, 111–13. *See also* Medicaid; Medicare; Social Security; *other government social transfer programs*
universal social programs, 18–19, 65, 66, 141. *See also* early education; health insurance; public education
university attendance. *See* higher education

vacations, paid, 28, 69, 111, 138
value added taxation (VAT). *See* consumption taxes
vested interests, 27, 141
Vishny, Robert W., 168n93
Voting Rights Act (1965), 11

wage insurance, 2, 18, 29
wages, 10, 22, 51, 132, 141, 149n80, 166n71; after-tax, 112, 116–18, 164n58, 165n65; female/male

ratios of, 52–53, 53; stagnant, 2, 25–28, 137. *See also* minimum wage
Wagner's law, 81, 83, 91
Washington, DC, 7
Wealth of Nations (Smith), 35
Weiss, Andrew, 155n5
welfare states, 36–66, 69, 111, 140–41, 150–51n4; anti-immigrant backlash in, 38; development of mother's human capital in, 52–54; Great Recession in, 54–55; health care systems in, 48–52; lack of evidence supporting conservative opposition to, 38–44, 106–7; population aging in, 37–38, 56–66; progress on social concerns in, 37, 44–45, 152n9; tax and transfer mix in, 46–48, 107–8, 115
Werker, Eric, 157n19
Wilhelm, Mark, 119
work hours, 8, 14, 111, 118. *See also* hours worked
work-life balance, 27, 62. *See also* paid parental leave
World Development Indicators, 157nn17,20, 161n35, 163n57, 167n83
World Economic Forum, 12–13
World Top Income Database, 167n83
World War II, 10, 51; postwar era, 24–26, 60, 86

Yellen, Janet, 27
Yergin, Daniel, 145n3

CPSIA information can be obtained
at www.ICGtesting.com
Printed in the USA
LVOW10s1823021216
515532LV00003B/438/P